Paul's SAT® Reading

Paul Kim

Copyright © 2019 Paul Academy All rights reserved.
ISBN: 979-11-86461-22-8
No part of this book may be reproduced without writtten permission from the author.
SAT is a registered trademark of the College Board, which is not affiliated with and does not endorse this product.
For more information, visit us at paulacademy.net

Copyright © 2019 by Paul Academy. All rights reserved.

ISBN: 979-11-86461-22-8

SAT is a registered trademark of the College Board, which does not sponsor or endorse this product.

Permission has been granted to reprint portions of the following:

Excerpt from "Is It Art or Knowledge? Deconstructing Australian Aboriginal Creative Making." Cameron, Elizabeth (2015). MDPI Arts: 4, 68-74; doi:10.3390/arts4020068

Excerpt from "Impacts of Beech Bark Disease and Climate Change on American Beech." Stephanson, Christopher A. and Coe, Natalie R. (2017) MDPI Forests: 8(5), 155; https://doi.org/10.3390/f8050155

Excerpt from "Influence of Amino Acids, Dietary Protein, and Physical Activity on Muscle Mass Development in Humans." Dideriksen K, Reitelseder S, Holm L. (2013) MDPI Nutrients: 5(3), 852-876; https://doi.org/10.3390/nu5030852

Excerpt from "Pre-Sleep Protein Ingestion to Improve the Skeletal Muscle Adaptive Response to Exercise Training" Trommelen, Jorn and Van Loon, Luc J.C (2016) MDPI Nutrients: 8(12), 763; https://doi.org/10.3390/nu8120763

Excerpt from "Noise in Schools: A Holistic Approach to the Issue" Woolner, Pamela and Hall, Elaine. (2010) Published in Int. J. Environ. Res. Public Health. MDPI: 7(8), 3255-3269; https://doi.org/10.3390/ijerph7083255

Excerpt from "What's in a Name?" Borkfelt, Sune. (2011) MDPI Animals: 1(1), 116-125; https://doi.org/10.3390/ani1010116

Excerpt from "'I Felt Like My Life Had Been Given to Me to Start Over': Alice Kaplan's Language Memoir, French Lessons" Rao, Eleonora. (2016) MDPI Humanities: 5(2), 47; https://doi.org/10.3390/h5020047

Excerpt from "Frog Swarms: Earthquake Precursors or False Alarms?" Grant, Rachel A. and Conlan, Hilary. (2013) MDPI Animals: 3, 962-977; doi:10.3390/ani3040962.

Excerpt from "Alcohol-Induced Blackout" Lee H, Roh S, Kim DJ. (2009) Published in Int. J. Environ. Res. Public Health. MDPI: 6(11), 2783-2792; https://doi.org/10.3390/ijerph6112783

Excerpt from "High status males invest more than high status females in lower status same-sex collaborators" Markovits H, Gauthier E, Gagnon-St-Pierre E, Benenson JF. (2017) PLoS ONE 12(9): e0185408. https://doi.org/10.1371/journal.pone.0185408

Excerpt from "Alternative Resources for Renewable Energy: Piezoelectric and Photovoltaic Smart Structures" Vatansever D, Siores E, Shah T. (2012) Intechopen, DOI: 10.5772/50570

Excerpt from "The nexus of oil, conflict, and climate change vulnerability of pastoral communities in Northwest Kenya" Schilling J, Locham R, Weinzierl T, ViVekananDa J., Scheffran J. (2015) Eldis Earth Syst. Dynam. Discuss. 6, 1163–1200. doi:10.5194/esdd-6-1163-2015

Excerpt from "Problematic Smartphone Use, Deep and Surface Approaches to Learning, and Social Media Use in Lectures" Rozgonjuk D, Saal K, Täht K. (2018) MDPI Int. J. Environ. Res. Public Health, 15(1), 92; https://doi.org/10.3390/ijerph15010092

Excerpt from "Language in the Wild—Living the Carnival in Social Media" Vigmo, Sylvi and Lantz-Andersson, Annika. (2014) MDPI Soc. Sci.: 3(4), 871-892; https://doi.org/10.3390/socsci3040871

Excerpt from "Differences in play can illuminate differences in affiliation: A comparative study on chimpanzees and gorillas" Cordoni G, Norscia I, Bobbio M, Palagi E (2018) PLoS ONE 13(3): e0193096. https://doi.org/10.1371/journal.pone.0193096

Paul's SAT® Reading

Paul Academy

Preface

The Tiger Mom's Secret Weapon
How Asian Students really achieve SAT success

While teaching the SAT, I hungered to find the same quality of SAT test questions as the real College Board test, because the practice questions of leading test prep companies were slightly different from the real thing. They didn't match the real content or they were just too easy. The difference was so big that I had a hard time accurately predicting my students' scores. I decided to make new SAT books with new principles for success.

1. Fully Comprehensive

I have created comprehensive vocabulary lists based on how frequently each word has appeared in previous tests. I didn't want students to be forced to purchase three or four vocabulary books in order to get all the information they needed, and I didn't want them to have to study words they would never need. My grammar book provides concise, efficient coverage of every grammar rule that has been tested, and contains 4 top-quality practice tests. My essay book has a full list of released questions and a strategy that quickly allows any student to reach their highest possible score. My math book focuses more on the advanced tactics for students wanting to perfect their scores to 800.

2. Question Difficulty Level: CollegeBoard

Previously, there were only a few prep books on the market aimed at Advanced Learners (scoring over 700 in each section), but even though the questions in the book were difficult, the skills they taught were irrelevant to success in the SAT. My book strictly adheres to the topics, skills, and reasoning that CollegeBoard actually tests.

3. Linking Concepts to Real CollegeBoard examples

When I explain a concept in my books, I find example questions in both the Official SAT guide and my own practice tests to drive the concept home. Students always know exactly what to expect and how to use what they are learning.

Using these three principles, my students' scores skyrocketed. I received many requests to make my strategies public, and so here now they are finally being printed. It has become the number one choice for reliable, comprehensive SAT success in the Asian market, and it will no doubt work for you, too.

Paul Kim

CONTENTS

1. Preface 4

2. Contents 5

3. How to Use This Book 6

4. Introduction to the SAT 7

5. Part I: General Strategies 11
   A. Multiple Choice Strategy 12
   B. Passage Types 16
   C. Understanding Paragraphs 18
   D. Things to Look For 21
   E. Improving Reading Comprehension 27

6. Part II: Individual Question Type Strategies 31
   A. Main Idea/Purpose/Detail... 32
   B. Inference: Don't Go Too Far 34
   C. Vocabulary in Context: Use Your Finger 36
   D. Line Evidence Questions: Q2 to Answer Q1 38
   E. Graph Questions: Pattern Hunter 46
   F. Time Management: MCSx2, Pick One, Move On 52

7. Practice Test 1 57

8. Practice Test 2 91

9. Practice Test 3 121

10. Practice Test 4 155

What's Inside

This book is a comprehensive reading strategy guide that will help you tackle even the most difficult SAT-style passage. In addition, this book also contains four full-length Reading Tests for the SAT, which we at Paul Academy have created based off the tests released by the College Board. These tests will simulate a real test and help you prepare for the actual exam.

How to Use This Book

If you have only a limited amount of time to prepare for the SAT, you should start with the practice tests immediately. When you get a question wrong, label it incorrect but do not write down the answer. Try to solve the question again. If you simply made a mistake, you should be able to correct your error. If you still have trouble, you may want to review the relevant concepts in the book. Review the concepts and take notes. Apply the strategy to your reading!

If you have plenty of time to prepare for the exam, start with the multiple choice strategy and process of elimination (POE) guides. These are the 2 main skills you need to achieve an excellent score on the SAT. When you solve practice questions, focus on the questions you got incorrect. Try to solve them again without looking at the answer. If you still have trouble, you may want to review the relevant concepts. Each question in the test is categorized, so you can find the chapter concepts quickly. Review the concept and take notes, then try the practice questions at the end of the chapter. When you're ready, take a full-length practice test.

And Lastly

Do not worry! The SAT may seem daunting at first, but you can prepare yourself to be ready on test day. Also, if you are in 11th grade or lower, you can always take the test again before you apply to college. In fact, studies have shown that most students score higher on their second try, so it is recommended that you take the test at least twice.

Introduction to the SAT

What You Need to Know About the Test

What is the SAT?

The SAT is an entrance exam used by most colleges and universities to make admissions decisions. It is a multiple choice, pencil-and-paper test administered by the College Board.

What's on the SAT?

The redesigned SAT is 3 hours long, or 3 hours and 50 minutes long if you choose to take the optional essay. It includes 4 timed sections (plus the essay).

Redesigned SAT			
Section	Exam length	Number of questions	Exam method
Reading	65min	52	4 LP 1 DP
Writing & Language	35min	44	4 Passages
Essay	50min	1	1 EP 1 RP
Math	80min	58	Calculator / 38 questions NO Calculator / 20 questions
Total	180min (230 min with essay)	154 (155 with essay)	

※LP: Long Passages, DP: Dual Passages, EP: Essay Prompt, RP: Reading Passage

Reading Section

The Reading Section is 65 minutes long and consists of 52 multiple-choice questions, all of which are passage-based.

There are a total of 4 passages and 1 dual passage in the Reading Section. The passages are excerpts from literature, science and social science articles and journals, and historical documents. In addition, 2-3 charts or graphs are included in the passages.

Writing & Language Section

The Writing & Language Section is 35 minutes long and consists of 44 multiple-choice questions.

There are a total of 4 passages in the Writing & Language Section. The passages cover a range of topics including history/social science, science, and career information.

Math Test

Range	Number of questions	Percentage of total questions
Heart of Algebra (Creating, Solving, Interpreting Linear Expressions)	21	36%
Problem Solving and Data Analysis	16	27%
Passport to Advanced Math (Quadratic/Exponential Functions)	15	26%
Additional Topics (Area/Volume Calculation, Investigation of Lines, Angles, Triangles and Circles Using Theorem, Working with Trigonometric Functions	6	11%
Total	58	100%

The Math Test is 80 minutes long and is divided into 2 sections: the Calculator Section and the NO Calculator Section. The NO Calculator Section is 25 minutes long and consists of 20 questions, including 5 student response questions, which are also known as grid-in questions. In them, you will be asked to write your answer and bubble in the appropriate numbers in the answer key. The Calculator Section is 55 minutes long and consists of 38 questions, including 8 grid-ins questions.

Classification	Question type	Exam length
Calculator	30 multiple choice 8 grid-ins	55minutes
NO calculator	15 multiple choice 5 grid-ins	25minutes
Total	58 questions	80minutes

Optional Essay

In the Essay Section of the exam, you will be asked to read a short passage and explain how the author effectively builds his or her argument. The key is to analyze the writer's rhetorical strategy, logic, and argument, and then put it into your own words.

Scoring Your Test

The redesigned SAT is scored on a scale of 400~1600. Each section of the SAT is graded separately, based on your raw score for each section. The optional essay is graded separately on a scale of 0 to 24.

1) Total Score (400~1600) = Evidence-Based Reading and Writing (200~800) + Math (200~800)
2) Essay (0~24) = Reading (0~8) + Writing (0~8) + Analysis (0~8)

Scoring Tips

Unlike previous versions of the SAT, there is no penalty for wrong answers. This means that you should always guess, even if you are unsure about the right answer. Also, there are only 4 answer choices in the current version of the SAT. Learning how to eliminate wrong answer choices quickly will be extremely beneficial.

How can I take the SAT?

The SAT schedule is available on the College Board website at www.collegeboard.org. You can sign up online or through mail using an SAT registration booklet.

It is important to register early for the exam as there may not be any spots available if you wait until the last minute.

Part I

General Strategies

1   Multiple Choice Strategy (MCS)

Following this strategy is the most important step in improving your score, no matter what score you are currently getting. Good technique and clear thinking when selecting your answers is the single most important skill to master. These strategies should be followed no matter what, regardless of the content of the question. If you are already following methods similar to this, then good, you don't need to change much. If don't do step 2 below before step 3, however, you are welcome for your new higher score.

1. First and most importantly, **read everything in the question carefully.**

It is easy with all of the nerves and panic of test day to feel pressure to read quickly. However, if you do not understand what a question is asking, you obviously cannot answer it. Be careful not to misread the question.

2. After reading the question, **decide on your own answer BEFORE** even **LOOKING** at the answer choices.

This is **extremely important** due to something called "confirmation bias." Take the following (possibly familiar) scenario:

- You read the question. Before deciding for yourself what the correct answer is, you allow the test to supply you with possible choices.
- You know that one of the four choices is correct, so -- with no reasoning at all -- you select one as the preliminary "right" answer.

"Confirmation bias" is the tendency for the human mind to fight against being proven wrong. Even when faced with the proof of its incorrect choice, the mind will fight back and rationalize its first, unconsidered, irrational choice.

Prevent this irrational choice by not making a 'first choice' based on what the answers give you.
Read the Question.
Form a **'First Choice' in your own words.**
<u>Only</u> **then** read the answer choices.

3. Once your answer has been decided, every other choice MUST be checked against the language given by the passage itself. This is otherwise known at good **Process of Elimination**. For every question with a reference to specific lines or details in the passage, you should consult the passage at least once in searching for an

answer. Go through each answer A - D and look for language in each one which is obviously wrong. Sometimes **a single wrong word will make an answer choice wrong.** Never finalize your choice without disproving all the other answers as well. There are many times where we are fooled and don't realize it until we have to disprove something we initially dismissed. Being confused can lead us to the correct answer.

5. If you get to two options, find the answer which seems less likely or which requires more proof and ask yourself the question "What do I need to see for this to be true?"

6. Return to the passage to double check for the right answer. If you don't find the extra information you need to justify the more complex answer, choose the more general one. Treat this as a general rule.

In fact, let's repeat that in slightly different terms to ensure we can use it / reference it again:

When faced with two options, take the less complex and/or the less extreme.

Our other "golden" rule is just as important:

All answers, even for inference based questions, can be found through direct reference to the passage itself.

If you haven't found proof for your answer, then you cannot be 100% sure you are correct, even if you have eliminated all the other options. The only response to improve this circumstance is read more, study vocabulary, and practice MCS.

Process of Elimination (PoE): Wrong Answer Categorization

For some people PoE is not complicated, but everyone can benefit from a system of how to categorize the reasons why a wrong answer is wrong. Fortunately, incorrect SAT answer choices follow a fairly predictable pattern and can be organized accordingly. For the below examples, you may choose to use them to label answer choices as you do PoE on the test if it does not take too much time.

1. NM - Not Mentioned - There is no mention of this topic in the passage
2. NI - Not the Issue - There is a mention of this topic in the passage, but it does not answer the question, or is the wrong focus for the question
3. 2Str - Too Strong - This word is too strong to be considered correct
4. 2Gen - Too General - This word is too general to be considered correct for the concepts in the passage
5. 2Spc - Too Specific - This word is too specific to be considered correct for the concepts in the passage
6. Opp - Opposite - This phrase is the opposite of whatever the correct answer is

7. Y - this part of the question is actually correct (part right, part wrong)

Examples

From hypothetical text:
"It can clearly be stated that the best course of action to preserve the environment is to drive less and conserve more."

Question: Which of the following best describes the author's primary recommendation for saving the environment?

The test could provide a number of possible wrong answers. Most incorrect answers would follow one of the patterns below:

NM: In order to reduce gas prices, we need to save fuel and use cars less.
In this case, *reducing gas prices* is "not mentioned". Multiple things in a question might be wrong, but you only need to find one wrong aspect of the question to highlight.

NI: Preserving the environment is an important task that we should do.
The fact that it is *important* is not the issue, the the question is about the primary recommendation, so the answer is wrong because it is "not the issue".

2Str: In order to preserve the environment, we must stop driving and never use fuel again.
The author does not go so far as to say we should stop *driving entirely* or *never use fuel again*, but less extreme versions of these concepts, making it wrong.

2Gen: In order to preserve the environment, we must take action in regard to automobiles.
The author does argue this, but the answer of *take action* is not specific enough to work as an acceptable answer.

2Spc: In order to preserve the environment, we must drive fewer trucks and cars, and preserve unleaded gasoline.
While the author mentions less driving and more fuel conservation, they do not specifically mention *trucks and cars* or *unleaded gasoline* so the answer is wrong.

Opp: In order to preserve the environment, we must drive more and conserve less.

Technically, this could also be listed as NM, but this happens so regularly that it can be simpler just to identify when the literal opposite of the correct answer is being used.

Y: In order to preserve the environment, we must **Y** <u>drive less</u> and conserve less.

Sometimes, the test will try to trick you by introducing an answer choice that is half right and half wrong. It can be helpful to identify where the answer choice is correct as well as where it is wrong.

2　Passage Types

Each test has a set number of various passage and question types so that preparing for it is easier. Here we will provide a breakdown of what to expect.

There are four content areas that will be present on each test in some form or another:

History   Social Science   Literature   Science

There will always be only **one** literature passage. There will always be **one** history passage. There will always be either **two social science passages and one science passage**, or **one social science passage and two science passages**.

One **dual passage** will be included on each test.

How the various types of passages present their information will change from test to test, but they appear to follow certain guidelines.

History/Social Science

History passages are taken from actual historical documents, so the style of language can be very difficult if you are not prepared. There are passages that come from more modern sources, but the considering the number of texts that come from people like Thomas Jefferson, it is important that you familiarize yourself with the style of writing from that time period.

Social science passages deal with things like government, society, and other social phenomena. They are almost always accompanied by graphs or charts, similar to science passages. Generally, you will need to be comfortable with a level of academic language and rhetoric similar to reading news from news sources like *The New York Times* or a magazine like *The New Republic*.

Literature

These passages can vary widely from test to test. Most often they are more challenging than on previous tests, and require the ability to read books like Jane Austen's *Pride and Prejudice*. The difficulty level can change, but nothing at a higher difficulty level than this has been printed in the test so far.

Science

These passages require reading skills similar to the skills needed for *history/social science* passages. However, the content of science passages is much more technical. Because of this, the language and grammar used is rarely very difficult. However, you will need to be able to identify the difference between important and unimportant information. You will also need to be able to use context to identify unknown vocabulary words and confusing terminology.

3. Understanding Paragraphs

Just as every passage has its own Main Idea and Tone, each paragraph has its own smaller main idea and smaller tone. It is at this level that you become able to create a map of the passage and quickly identify the location of details when a question asks you to identify them.

Take a look at the paragraph below:

> The main purpose of T.S. Eliot's poem "The Wasteland" is to combine and harmonize traditional narrative forms with the experimentation that his fellow Modernists were fond of. If the reader only thinks of Eliot as a "modernist," then it is simple to find support for this idea in the poem. But Eliot's actual purpose is to not only to do away with traditional storytelling in favor of the new, modernist method. His larger goal was to integrate the new style into the mythologies of the old so that both might be fresh again.

There is a lot going on here, but before we figure anything else out compared to the rest of the passage, we need to figure out this paragraph's reason for existing. One trick that works very often is to **look at the first and last sentences of the paragraph.** Usually you want to read the whole passage, but for the purpose of figuring out the main idea of a paragraph, this is a good way to remove confusing or extra material. If you are running out of time on the section, these may be the only things you have time to read.

If we follow this advice, we can clearly see that the main idea is that **T.S. Eliot wanted to combine old and new styles in ""The Wasteland."** On your test paper, you could record that in the margins as "**Eliot wanted combine old/new**" or any shorthand that works for you to remember all the important details. Since there isn't a lot of time, it is sometimes better to simply take a moment and make an internal note.

There isn't much emotion or persuasion going on, so the tone would be **neutral**, and you would not need to write it down unless you wanted to.

Now that you have a handle on paragraph summary, try to predict what will come next in the passage. Thinking ahead gives you perspective and helps you see what the author is doing. Given the information in this paragraph, do you think you can predict what will come from the rest of the passage?

If this is the first paragraph of the passage, the next paragraph would likely be an explanation of exactly *how* Eliot managed to combine the old and new in his poem. There might be quotes from the poem, or quotes from an English professor, or a quote from ancient Greece, but regardless it is going to be about the fusion mentioned in the introduction paragraph.

Example: Try identifying the purpose of the following paragraph:

> Betsy Fowler slowly came to accept her new situation, and even to enjoy herself at parties with the other housewives of the neighborhood. They would all gossip cheerfully over coffee and share middle class problems in blandly decorated living rooms. These rooms required so little maintenance that it was even possible to get by without a maid. Despite her husband's diminished income, Betsy relished the common role she had fallen to and seldom looked back fondly on the privileges of wealth. Considering the difficulties her family had been through during the last year, it was much easier now to discern what was truly valuable.
>
> **What does the first sentence tell us?**
>
>
>
>
> **What other information can we glean from the rest of the paragraph?**
>
>
>
>
> **What can we guess may be the focus of the passage?**

Once we get through the first sentence, most of the rest of the paragraph is simply expanding on that idea. We see immediately that the character mentioned (this is a narrative passage) and her family have lost a lot of money and social standing, but she remains upbeat.

Your main idea might be something like: "Betsy's family is in a bad place, but she is optimistic."

The rest of the passage may reflect this idea. Of course, it may not, but that's the sort of mystery we'll be exploring in the other paragraphs. At least, for now, we have a possible starting point to guide our reading.

> NOTE: On this issue, keep in mind that the rest of the passage may NOT follow the first paragraph, and that, instead, the beginning offers a contradictory view to that presented in the rest of the passage. Perhaps make a mark like "+" or "–" to keep track of which paragraphs support the main idea and which are against it.

4   Things to Look For

On some passage types, particularly those concerned with science or drier sections of history, our minds seem to wander, leaving us with that horrible feeling of "did I really understand that?" which requires us to reread the passage and waste time that we don't have. Therefore, our problem is: How do we **keep our attention focused** on the passage?

One strategy might be to just read lots of boring material for hours a day, slowly grinding away your joy in life and your love of learning until you are a dry shell of a human being, unable to do anything but scratch meaning from SAT texts.

Another, better way would be to give yourself **challenges** while reading to keep your mind occupied on the task at hand. After all, how can one be distracted when one has a mystery to solve every time one picks up a passage?

The mystery is larger than a game however, as the details and Things that follow here are overwhelmingly the Things that questions are based on. If you can become an expert in identifying lists and what they are listing, or immediately spotting a contrasting pair, or seeing a Transition Word and knowing that you need to be looking for a changing idea, then you are well on your way to your best possible score.

So here are some Things to keep an eye out for among the less important information in each passage.

A. Problems / Questions / Terms (P/Q/T)

Things that need to be solved, answered, or defined

Whenever there is a question, problem, or passage-specific term in the passage, you should make it your task to find the answer, solution, or definition before the end.

> Criminologists have long connected the decline of violent crime in modern times with improvements in police work. In this theory, the "broken windows" method of policing, in which even minor offenses are punished swiftly, led to a gradual removal of the urban decay which allowed for the high crime rates of the 1970s and 80s. But just how much credit can these

policies take for the sudden drop in violent crime which began in the 1990s? A recent study suggests that the true hero of the tale may not be law enforcement at all, but rather environmental protection.

Here we have a perfect example of a question at the beginning of the passage. This sort of question really frames the passage and focuses our attention. We know, in short, what the main idea is, almost without reading the rest of the passage.

Which of the following could be a possible answer to the question posed in the passage?

> A. People should always follow the instructions of police officers
> B. Levels of law enforcement appear to have little impact on crime rates
> C. The legal system is corrupt

Obviously, if something like the second option (B) comes up, we should immediately notice it and add it to our understanding of the main idea of the passage. The primary question asked in the first paragraph of the passage has been answered! It must be important.

B. "Quotes"

Whenever the author introduces a quote from another source, our **main task** is to ask ourselves "**How does this relate** to the passage's overall point? Does it agree? From what perspective is it addressing the main issue?"

Three reasons for quotation marks:
Citation
Introducing new words
Sarcastic, "so-called" tone

Look at the quotation marks in line 3. What is meant by putting the word "progress" in quotes?

> The beginning of the age of Enlightenment brought with it the beginning of the mythology that surrounds the idea of "progress." At first the idea of progress served to counter the stagnancy and decay of existing European social systems. Writers like Voltaire and Diderot began to legitimize challenges to the old and corrupt regimes of France and other nations, which had long been dominated by royal and religious excess. An obsession with

progress later drove discussions of "utopia" and other visions of an endlessly improving future. This focus on forward motion finally culminated in the "idealism" and excesses of the American and French revolutions. This ideology extends even to the present. The holiness of the idea of progress in modern scientific and religious circles protects those who claim to wage war in the name of democracy, the sister idea to advancement.

How might the quotation marks in lines 2 and 9 be different?

For the first set of quotation marks, it's clear that there is no one in the passage to quote from, so it could not be a citation. Likewise, it couldn't be a new term, since the word discovered is not unusual or mysterious. As such, it seems clear that the passage intends for us to see that the author is not using the word "progress" in the typical sense of the word. Therefore we could interpret this as a sarcastic or at least skeptical use of the phrase, especially given the usage of the word "mythology."

As for the second use of the marks, the mention of "other visions of the future" in lines 9 and 10, the quotation marks seem to reflect the views of the Enlightenment thinkers, and as such could be interpreted as **citations**, or perhaps as **introductions of new terms.**

C. Contrasting Pairs

A = B; A ≠ B; Thought it was A? Actually, it's B

These are "sets" of terms, people, or any other elements the author wishes to compare for some reason. These items are usually opposites and are used to help define each other. They are especially useful for identifying key **tensions** in the passage, and help us understand specific concepts by presenting us with their opposites.

When we see contrasts, we should make note of them and possibly mark them in a way that identifies where there are two opposing concepts in the passage. A quick line between the two might save you some time later. Once we've noted such contrasts, we should ask the following:

* What is the value (*good/bad*) of each part of the pair?
* Which does the author favor/prefer?

Obviously, the second question is not always relevant to the issues at hand and so could be replaced by "Which is most important in the context of the passage?"

Remember the T.S. Eliot passage from Chapter 2? We noted its pair of terms but we didn't establish what their significance might be in the larger passage. Let's refresh our memories and see if we can glean any extra information.

> The main purpose of T.S. Eliot's poem "The Wasteland" is to combine and harmonize traditional narrative forms with the experimentation that his fellow Modernists were fond of. If the reader only thinks of Eliot as a "modernist," then it is simple to find support for this idea in the poem. But Eliot's actual purpose is to not only to do away with traditional storytelling in favor of the new, modernist method. His larger goal was to integrate the new style into the mythologies of the old so that both might be fresh again.

As we noted then, the idea of combining the two styles is an important one, which should immediately alert us to the presence of a contrast. To summarize, we might write down "classical vs. modernist view."

For the rest of the passage we should be aware that the author will be drawing on these two terms as polarities between which, it would appear, Eliot attempted to situate himself. Future paragraphs may spend time talking about his modernist tendencies, and others his classical. In any event, we can easily anticipate a question in which the test may ask us something like "In the first paragraph, the author makes a distinction between____" to which we now have an easy answer without much further consultation needed.

D. Transition words

Indicate a movement/pivot from one concept/argument to the next

For the purpose of analyzing the intent of the passage, it is vital to note turning points which indicate a narrative shift between subjects or between two contrasting views, etc. There are many of these words, but here are a few of the most common:

However	Furthermore
But	On the other hand
Nevertheless	Of course... (suggests new topic after a concession)
While...	Unlike...
Conversely	Specifically...(moving from general to specific)
Moreover	Yet

They can be easy to overlook. Don't overlook them! The entire meaning of a paragraph can turn on a big fat "But," "Yet," or "However." Have a keen eye for them and never let one escape you.

E. Lists

Series, checklists, catalogues and inventories

Whenever the passage gives a list of reasons, varying types of some element, or terms to contrast in the passage, we should make note of them, as there may be questions about the list itself, or particular elements of it, for which we should be prepared. The more the list seems to be referenced in the passage, and the longer the passage spends on each element, then more attention we should pay to it.

> The habitat of blue whales extends throughout almost all the oceans of the planet. This includes the Atlantic, the Pacific and the Indian, all the way south to the banks of Antarctica, though the animals are excluded from the icy reaches of the Arctic. Despite the sprawling expanse of their domain, the largest vertebrate creatures in the history of the planet struggle to remain in existence. A number of factors contribute to this decline. Whaling is responsible for the initial decimation of blue whale populations, with the numbers plummeting to as few as 500 animals in the 1960s from pre-industrial whaling estimates of more than 250,000. Apart from outright hunting, commercial shipping poses the largest threat to the survival of blue whales. While the animals are amongst the fastest and strongest creatures in the ocean, they are still unable to evade transport ships if their paths happen to cross and end up mauled by the ships' propellers. Sonar used by these vessels also interferes with blue whales' ability to communicate with other members of their species. Studies show that in the presence of sound frequencies in the range utilized by sonar equipment, blue whale frequencies cease at once and do not resume until long after the ships have passed. This disruption likely stymies efforts at mating and socialization, further inhibiting efforts to revitalize the population. World prohibitions on whaling and increased knowledge of the migratory patterns of the blue whale mitigate the effects of these problems, but marine biologists still fear that it may be too late to turn back the tide of extinction.

While this part of the passage is very difficult to separate with use of transition words, it is far too large to leave without segmenting it somehow. However, language like "a number of factors" mentioned in line 9 should alert us to the presence of a **list**, making it possible for us to separate it into several parts, all of which might be considered "reasons for endangerment."

5. Improving Reading Comprehension

It is important to read the whole passage when taking the SAT. Reading everything allows your mind the time and space to make the connections you need to answer the questions they will ask. Get good at recognizing the important parts of passages as you read. While this may seem like a waste of time at first glance, the truth is that since many of the reading questions are simply locating and identifying details, if you properly analyze the passage while you read it, it will ultimately *save* you time.

In order to understand a passage, we need to know *what* is important. What is important in a passage is determined by the author's intentions, so that is the most important question we want to answer:

Why is the author writing this?

This question does not have to be answered right away, but if you can't answer this question confidently by the end of the passage, you do not have full comprehension of the passage.

Of all the 'W' questions you can ask about a passage, 'Why' is the most important. You might easily be able to figure out 'What' an author is writing about (whales, for example), but unless you know *why* she is writing about whales, you won't be fully comprehending the reading.

There are three reasons an author will be writing a passage for the SAT:

1. **Inform**
2. **Persuade**
3. **Entertain**

The point in listing these broad generalizations is to draw attention to the wide variety of ways in which an author can go about doing these things.

If the author wants to **Inform** her audience about whales, she could employ anything from neutral, detached scientific reporting to personal anecdotes that reveal her deep personal connection to the subject. Information is not always neutral, but a point of view does not necessarily mean an author is trying to persuade.

> "Whales are the largest animals on earth."
> ⇒ informative and neutral

> "Whales are the largest animals on earth, and the most beautiful."
> ⇒ informative and pro-whale

> "Whales are the largest animals on earth, and I hate large animals."
> ⇒ informative and anti-whale

If the author wishes to **Persuade** her audience about whales, then she will inform them and argue in favor or against a particular action or way of thinking. Again, this could be done with a dry, neutral tone:

> "Whales must be saved in order preserve the balance of the ecosystem, without which human society may perish."
> ⇒ Action advocated (save the whales), no emotional words

Or, it could be done in a humorous way:

> "Ask a whale why it should be saved and it could quite easily turn around and ask you the same question about humans."
> ⇒ ironic tone indicates that the author's advocates saving the whale by implying an argument about the value of all life.

Usually the Social Science, History, and Science passages will be either informative or persuasive. The Literature passages will most often be written for Entertainment purposes.

If the author wishes to **Entertain** her readers, as in a fictional passage, then the questions of *how* and *why* an author is writing is less important than figuring out *what* is happening, *who* it is happening to, and *where*, *when*, *why* and *how* it is happening. Basically, transfer your consideration about the author's intentions to those of the characters in the story.

For all passages, roughly speaking, once you have determined **Why** the author is writing, you have determined **the Main Idea** of the passage.

When you have determined **How** the author is writing, you have determined **the Tone** of the passage.

Without both of these understandings in your possession, you cannot be certain that you have fully comprehended the passage. Write them at the top of the page. There is almost always a question that specifically relates to the Main Idea, and if the Tone is anything but neutral, there will likely be a question about that as well.

Here is a rough guide to where some of the most common tone words fall on a spectrum of possible options. If you are faced with a passage that seems more extreme, then obviously consult those listed under the 'high' heading. When in doubt, **the less extreme answer is *usually* the correct answer.**

Low positivity

Amused

Animated

Nostalgic / Wistful

Reflective

Sympathetic

Tolerant

Whimsical

High positivity

Awestruck

Amazed

Idealistic

Delighted

Neutrality

Analytical

Confiding

Curious

Cynical / Wry / Dry / Irony / Sarcasm / Sardonic

Dramatic / Melodramatic

Indifferent

Tentative

Scholarly

Low negativity

Ambivalent

Apathetic

Apologetic

Baffled

Defensive

Disbelieving

Disillusioned / Jaded / Disenchanted

Envious

Feigning interest

Grudging

Judgmental

Patronizing / Condescending

Presumptuous

Provocative

Puzzled

Resigned

Skeptical

Weary

High negativity

Appalled

Contemptuous

Defiant

Disconsolate

Disdainful

Dismayed

Hostile

Offended

Outraged

Resentful

Righteous

Indignant

Shocked

Part II

Individual Question Type Strategies

1 | Main Idea/Purpose/Detail

These three question types are grouped together because they all involve the same skill: finding support for the correct answer literally within the text. There is nothing fancy going on, no logical deductions to make or tricks to avoid. Here are some tips for dealing with these kinds of questions efficiently.

A. Main Idea/Purpose Questions

Example: *"The primary purpose of the passage is to..."*

If you read the whole passage, these should be fairly easy, but it is not always necessary to read the whole passage to answer these questions. Especially for science and social science passages, a skilled reader can go with a "First and Last" approach. Read the first and last paragraphs of the passage, as well as the first and last sentences of each other paragraph. Very often, this will be enough information for you to be able answer questions like the one above.

One major exception to the "First and Last" technique are literary passages. It is nearly impossible to figure out what is going on just by scanning fiction. There is no avoiding the need to read the entirety of the literary passage. However, here are some things to look for while you read that should help isolate the most important information that will be required to answer the questions:

Who are the "characters"?
Even if there is just one woman lost on a boat in the ocean, the ocean itself could conceivably be considered a character, or a mother back home whom the daughter is thinking of. Keep track of every "character" that is important.

What are their relationships?
In our previous example, we might imagine that the woman on the boat is a "prisoner" of the ocean since she is trying to get away. The relationship between the woman and her mother is fairly clear, unless the woman on the boat had a fight with her mother and they are no longer speaking. These details are important to fully comprehending what is going on in a story and to having the right information for the questions.

What does everybody want?
Once the relationships are established, figure out what each of the characters wants, either from other

characters or the world. In our woman on a boat story, perhaps the woman wants to escape the ocean and reconnect with her mother. We wouldn't know what the mother wanted, and the ocean doesn't have any desires, so the main idea of the passage would be that "A woman on a boat in the ocean wants to go home and reconnect with her mother."

B. Other Purpose Questions

Example: *"Within the context of the passage, Paragraph 2 serves to..."*
"The author most likely references 'big mistakes' in line 33 in order to..."

Both of the above examples deal with the purpose of a specific portion of the passage, rather than the passage as a whole. In these more specific situations, you may need to dig deeper and read the entire paragraph. Otherwise the strategies are the same.

C. Detail Questions

"According to the passage, the primary cause of increased carbon dioxide is..."

Detail questions are ones that require you to identify only specific details as they are presented in the passage. The only thing you have to be able to do is actually locate the information and interpret it, and you will be fine. One effective method for locating necessary information is to look for something striking about the information you are looking for, such as "dioxide" (an unusual word) in the above example, or, say the "ookkee" in ""bookkeeper." Focusing on these small identifiers will allow you to scan the passage and ignore irrelevant information.

2 Inference: Don't Go Too Far

Example: *"Which of the following can be inferred from the author's reference to 'a big mistake' in line 33?"*

Inference is simply reaching a conclusion based on evidence and reasoning. For example, what can be accurately inferred from the answer to this question?

"Are you hungry?"
"I had lunch just 20 minutes ago."

    Can it be inferred that
    1. I am not hungry?
    2. I will not join you if you ask?
    3. I usually have lunch at this time?
    4. I am upset that you asked?

It is possible to argue that all of these are *possible*, but only number 1 is actually able to be inferred from the answer, since the question asked is "Are you hungry?", and when one eats it is reasonable to assume that they eat until they are no longer hungry. If the question was "Would you like to go to lunch?", then number 2 would be a possible answer. If the answer was "I have lunch at 12" then 3 would be possible, and if the answer was "No!" then 4 would be possible. Small changes in context and information change what is possible to be inferred.

Practice with the following paragraph:

Crack! Thunder struck and rain poured. Jim stared blankly out the window, trying to contain his emotions that raged like the weather. He was beginning to lose it. Dropping the kite from his hand, Jim broke out into full sob. His mother comforted him, "There, there, Jim. We'll just find something else to do." She began to unpack the picnic basket that was on the counter and offered him a sandwich. Jim snapped, "I don't wanna sandmich!" A flash from the sky lit up the living room. *Boom!* Mom sighed.

"Let's try to answer some questions:"

1. Why is Jim upset?
2. What was Jim planning on doing today?
(Look at the bottom of the page for answers)

Stay "within the lines". Inference only applies to what is in the text!

1. he wanted to fly a kite, but it is raining / 2. go on a picnic

3   Vocabulary in Context: Use Your Finger

Vocabulary questions are the easiest questions in theory, as they can be answered by using only one sentence from the passage, but somehow they often rank among the most difficult for even top students, because of their use of obscure or secondary definitions of words.

When you see a vocabulary question, make a special effort NOT to look at the answer options. Doing so will adversely color your opinion of the word before we look back at the word as it appears in the passage.

Now, to best answer a vocabulary question, we should cover up the word in question as we read.

When we read the sentence again, we should think of a synonym for the word as close as possible to its use in the sentence, and either write that down or keep repeating it to ourselves as we return to the answer choices.

Choose the word that is closest in meaning to the word you have selected yourself.

Example:

> *Every week on Friday we have art class in the school annex, which is closer to the school's exit. If a kid can get to the bus before the others, he or she is rewarded with a prime position at the back. Once the bell rings, the students burst from the art room doors like a pack of loosed hounds and careen* **helter-skelter** *down the hall. In the brouhaha, a loose locker door bangs into my knee. I cry out in pain and hobble out the door, barely missing a step.*
>
> 16. As used in the passage, "helter-skelter" (line 7) most nearly means
> (A) mindlessly
> (B) recklessly
> (C) rapidly
> (D) furiously

Looking at the options, it seems like we have a difficult choice, but if we remember our own choice of "wildly" and "irresponsibly" we know that we should go with B, as "recklessly" is a perfect combination of those two words.

Don't spend too much time thinking it over. This is one case where your intuition is usually correct, as long as you are familiar with the words involved. Choose the option that best suits your initial guess and move on. The wrong answer choices are chosen specifically to make you doubt yourself in these cases, so it is best not to play their game.

4 | Line Evidence Questions: Q2 to Answer Q1

At first, these huge double questions with their multiple line references and confusing relationships can be quite intimidating. But there's no need to worry. If you follow a slightly modified Multiple Choice Safety plan that we established earlier, these questions are arguably EASIER than an individual detail or inference-based question. Line reference questions look like this:

26. According to the passage, which of the following best represents the opinion of Lord Farthington about the value of engaging in international trade?
    A. It is good.
    B. It is bad.
    C. It is terrible.
    D. It is amazing.

27. Which of the following best provides evidence for the previous question?
    A. Lines 10-12 (For the benefit...trampoline.)
    B. Lines 17-29 (I sat by...Norwegian wood.)
    C. Lines 30-31 (Picture yourself...marmalade skies.)
    D. Lines 36-39 (International trade...is good.)

For the purpose of SAT, learn to scan all of the questions in a section passively so you can recognize when you are dealing with a dual question like this. Once you have spotted one, treat it like a normal question in terms of Multiple Choice Strategy, with the following exception:

After reading and understanding the question (MCS Step 1), use the line reference question to find your own answer (Step 2) instead of doing it by yourself.

Example: Let's take a look at the following passage and questions.

> More than worth its weight in gold, this royal-hued flower has spread its fragrance into every civilization and continent around the world. Spawning palace frescoes, therapeutic drugs, verses from Ovid, rich garments, and liquid perfumes, saffron has been greatly prized by people of every class and culture. It was mixed into the royal baths of Cleopatra to assist her in lovemaking, but it was also carried in the pouches of commoners and townsfolk
> 5 to ward off the unwelcome scent of perspiring fellow travelers. It was used to celebrate the arrival of military men - Nero entered Rome on a road carpeted with scattered saffron; however, it was also the mascara of fashionable women, who smeared it plentifully on their eyelashes for beauty. In the Song of Solomon, a beautiful lover's cheeks are compared to an orchard of "rare fruits, spikenard, and saffron," while Alexander the Great drank saffron tea and consumed saffron-sprinkled rice. Wan Zhen, a Chinese medical expert, also referred to saffron as both an offering to
> 10 the Buddha and an ingredient in wine. It was in post-classical Europe, however, that this modest flower blossomed with the most glorious, though short-lived, brilliance.
>
> 1. The author indicates that in ancient times, saffron was perceived mostly as
> (A) a source of foul smells.
> (B) a needless expense.
> (C) a sign of beauty.
> (D) a valuable commodity.
>
> 2.. Which choice provides the best evidence for the answer to the previous question?
> (A) Lines 2-3 ("Spawning ... culture.")
> (B) Lines 5-7 ("It ... beauty.")
> (C) Lines 7-9 ("In ... rice.")
> (D) Lines 10-11 ("It ... brilliance.")

First, we read the question and understand that we are looking for information on the perception of saffron in ancient times. Instead of going to the passage and trying to find it ourselves, we simply go straight to question 2 and let the test do the work for us.

In 2(A), we know that saffron was prized, which is a perception of saffron, so this is a promising candidate for the right answer.

In 2(B), we know where and how it was used, but we don't have textual evidence of people's opinion of it, only what we can infer. This is a tempting answer, but it isn't direct evidence and 2(A) is better anyway.

In 2(C), we know again how it was used. If 2(C) is right, 2(B) is right, so this takes them both out of contention.

In 2(D), we are given only information about when it was popular, not what people thought of it.

Our best option is 2(A), which tells us it is "prized," so let's go back to 1 and see what we can find.

1(A) is negative, prized is strongly positive, so this answer is wrong.

1(B) is negative, so it is also wrong

1(C) is positive, and a tempting answer, but we just know that people thought it was worth money, not specifically a sign of beauty. A closer look at the text shows there is no specific mention of it as a sign of beauty, but thankfully we don't have to worry about that since we have to work with Question 2 lines anyway, and nothing there provides evidence that "saffron = beauty." Rather, have "saffron = prized" and "prized = valued," therefore

1(D) is the correct answer.

A. Synonyms and Keywords

After you choose an answer for the previous question, it is important to look for **synonyms** in the answer choices for the line evidence question. Synonyms are words that have the same meaning. Looking for synonyms is often the quickest and most accurate way to find your answer.

If the answer for the previous question was "Sparse population of beluga whales," then that's your first clue! Search the lines for synonyms and keywords. "Sparse population of beluga whales" can be referred to in many different ways, such as "the decreasing number of these beautiful cetaceans," "the meager remnants of this threatened species," and so on. They all basically mean the same thing! Search carefully for the keywords in your line choices, and make sure that your line has words that are similar to the answer choice in your previous question.

B. Relationship to Subject

Sometimes ALL of the answer choices will contain keywords or synonyms of the answer to the previous question, and therefore none of the answers can be eliminated. In this case, you should examine the content of the lines and ask yourself if they are **relevant** to the subject (= answer to the previous question). Find the main idea of the line and see if it matches the subject. Does the line even mention the subject at all? If the line does mention the subject, what is its **relationship to the subject**? Eliminate the answer choices that are 1) IRRELEVANT to the subject 2) RELEVANT but have the wrong relationship with the subject.

For example, let's say that the previous question asked how the author feels about apples, and your answer was "He likes them." Look at the answer choices in the line evidence question, and eliminate answers that refer to lines in the passage that don't mention apples at all. Then eliminate the answers that refer to lines that say "Apples are bad."

Pay attention to the subject of the sentence in the grammatical sense as well. In most cases, the grammatical subject of the sentence = subject, or main idea of the sentence. This should help you find the relevant lines more quickly.

C. Tips

1. Tone

Looking at the tone of the answer choices in the previous question can often be helpful. If all of the answer choices have a **negative** tone, such as "global catastrophe," "warmongering," or "environmental disaster," then this gives us a clue to the next question. Check all of the answer choices in the line evidence question. Do some of them have a positive tone? Good! That means you can **eliminate the positive answers** in the line evidence question, because then they wouldn't qualify as evidence for any of the previous answer choices.

Think of it in the opposite way. If all of the choices had a **positive** tone, using words such as "pleasant surprise," "prized gift," or "increased appreciation," then we can **eliminate the negative answers** in the line evidence question.

2. Correcting Wrong Answers

If none of the choices in the line evidence question support your previous answer, that means you probably got the previous answer incorrect. Uh-oh! Don't worry, though: just go back to your previous question and read it over again carefully. If there is an answer that is better supported by one of the lines provided, change your answer to that instead.

Example: Let's read on and solve two more questions.

> As the Black Death ravaged Europe, saffron became more than simply a costly luxury: it became a universally sought panacea, as well as a preventative ingredient. Unfortunately, the local suppliers of saffron literally died out just when it was most in demand: farmers usually had their souls reaped before they could reap the produce of their crops. The Crusades cut off another source of supply (the prosperous Muslim lands), and the limited amount of
> 5 saffron in comparison to the demand made the delicate flower's prices escalate to perilous numbers. Nobles of old blood fought battles with the rising class of merchants over this precious spice, and adulteration by immersing saffron in honey, marigolds, or water was punished swiftly and painfully with immolation. Pirates, recognizing the immense value of this fragile spice, ignored ships full of gold to attack ships carrying saffron.

3. The author indicates that the cause of saffron's skyrocketing demands can be traced to
(A) an abundance in supply
(B) a catastrophic plague
(C) its symbol as a conflict between nobles and merchants
(D) less subjection to regulations

4. Which choice provides the best evidence for the answer to the previous question?
(A) Lines 1-2 ("As ... ingredient.")
(B) Lines 4-5 ("The ... numbers.")
(C) Lines 5-7 ("Nobles ... immolation.")
(D) Lines 7-8 ("Pirates ... saffron.")

Q3 Answer Key : (B)

(A) and (C) are obviously not true. In the passage, it states the very opposite. Saffron was scarce in supply because too many of the farmers were dying out, and it was subject to very strict regulations. Besides, neither of these are causes for saffron's increased demand.

(D) is also not true, because while it was true that nobles and merchants came into sharp conflict over saffron, the passage does not mention anything about saffron being a symbol of such conflict; besides, this detail is too specific.

Therefore, (B) is the correct answer.

Q4 Answer Key : (A)

Let's try the **synonym strategy:**

If you selected the answer to the previous question correctly, Question 4 should be easy for you. Pick the line which specifically mentions a similar phrase to "a catastrophic plague!" In this case, it would be lines 1-2, where it mentions how Black Death ravaged post-Classical Europe. Other similar phrases could be "contagious disease," "epidemic," or "pestilence."

Therefore, (A) is the correct answer.

B. Relationship to Subject

Example: Read the following passage from an excerpt of an 18th-century novel.

Upon the dissolution of her marriage, Lady Wintergreen thought it but proper to confer with her husband on the care of their only child, a daughter who remained the only consolation to both. "She wishes to stay with me, although I have informed her of your wishes," she stated, in one of her characteristic lavender-scented, neatly pressed letters. "I believe it would be best for us to come to an agreement in her presence; it is the least we can do
5 for this poor child." Sir Thomas Wintergreen, however, without the wit to preserve his marriage to a woman with rather too much of that quicksilver quality, did not have enough to accept this proposal amiably. His daughter had always pressed for open, mutual discussion in the family home, and it was quite plausible that she really desired to air their wounds in her hearing. But to meet her mother again - the woman who had shattered the comfortable monotony of his life - the woman who had the insolence to walk out of the house in the face of all decency, all
10 convention! - no, it was really asking too much. The lethargy of his slow intellect was so alarmed by this proposal, he took the tremendous effort to actually think, and to pen a letter in his own hand. "I will send a servant to fetch the child," he wrote at last, "and you may not accompany her. The child is mine by right; and if you refuse to send her, I shall press all the charges that I have hitherto left untouched."

1. The narrator portrays Sir Thomas Wintergreen as
(A) enraged.
(B) complacent.
(C) bereaved.
(D) foolish.

2. Which choice provides the best evidence for the answer to the previous question?
(A) Lines 1-2 ("Upon ... both.")
(B) Lines 6-8 ("His ... hearing.")
(C) Lines 8-10 ("But ... much.")
(D) Lines 10-11 ("The ... hand.")

Q1 Answer Key : (D)

(A) is not true, because there is no mention of Sir Thomas being angry, although his words can come off as unpleasant.

(B) is not true: there is no mention of Sir Thomas being self-satisfied.

(C) is not true. Although he doesn't seem happy with his separation from his wife, that is not the main focus of the narrator's portrayal of Sir Thomas. He is more alarmed by Lady Wintergreen's proposal than sorrowful over his loss.

The passage talks about how Sir Thomas was "without wit" and found it difficult to think; therefore, (D) is the correct answer.

Q2 Answer Key : (D)

Let's look at the **relationship to the subject**!

The subject in question is Sir Thomas Wintergreen. The question is asking about his personality.

First, let's eliminate the answer choices that are IRRELEVANT to the subject.

(A) is about *Lady* Wintergreen, not her husband. Out!

(B) is about his *daughter*. Out!

The remaining choices, (C), and (D), are relevent to Sir Thomas Wintergreen. (C), however, doesn't reveal much about his foolishness. It mostly shows how much he dislikes the idea of meeting Lady Wintergreen again. Therefore, this answer is **relevant**, but has a **weak relationship** with the subject.

(D) is both **relevant** to and has a **strong relationship** with the subject (Sir Thomas's thinking skills). "The lethargy of his slow intellect" shows that the narrator considers Sir Thomas pretty dumb; the narrator's mocking tone in describing how it required a huge effort just to think and actually write a letter reconfirms that idea. The correct answer is (D).

Example: Okay, let's read on.

When Lady Wintergreen received this letter, she called her daughter and said, "My dear, in every feeling that earthly affection prompts, and every impulse that duty requires, I am confident I would not waver. But my situation is a very unpleasant one, and wealth and fortune have never been my friends. Perhaps your father is right, and it is better that you return to him."

5   Lady Wintergreen was deeply attached to Cordelia, and often fancied her best self revived in her daughter. Just as Cordelia had been the one person to whom Sir Thomas softened with benevolence, she was the dearest object of her mother's sole care, as well as her greatest source of comfort. In every distress, without flattering the weaknesses of her mother or criticizing her unjustly, Cordelia would sit by her side shedding tears of silent sympathy; in every fleeting cause of joy, Cordelia lit up her mother's life with the effusions of youthful delight

10 which she gave vent to. In this instance, as in every other, Cordelia instantly caught the real meaning of her mother's words; and smiling a little sorrowfully, she responded: "Do not send me away, Maman; I will speak to the servant myself if he comes, and persuade him that I cannot leave. I need you." When really, both of them knew that Cordelia meant, you need me more than Father does.

3. According to the narrator, Cordelia comforts her mother by

(A) offering extensive, objective advice without taking the side of either parent.

(B) supporting her mother with constant encouragement and compliments.

(C) tempering her mother's mercurial moods with her calmness.

(D) wordlessly understanding her mother's feelings.

4. Which choice provides the best evidence for the answer to the previous question?

(A) Lines 1-2 ("When ... waver")

(B) Lines 5-7 ("Just ... comfort")

(C) Lines 7-10 ("In ... to")

(D) Lines 12-13 ("When ... does")

Q3 Answer Key : (D)

(A) is not true, because the passage states that Cordelia shed tears of "silent" sympathy.

(B) is false, because the passage implies that Cordelia did not compliment her mother much at all, as she never "flattered the weaknesses" of her mother.

(C) is not true. The passage does not say that Lady Wintergreen is mercurial (quickly changing in mood), and neither does it talk about Cordelia being especially calm. On the contrary, Cordelia cries with her mother and lets out "effusions of youthful delight."

(D) is the correct answer.

Q4 Answer Key : (C)

Once again, we can use the **subject relationship strategy**!

The subject in Question 3 was Cordelia, and how she comforts her mother (by wordlessly understanding her feelings). (C), where Cordelia sheds tears of silent sympathy for her mother without either complimenting or criticizing her, is the best evidence for the previous answer.

(A) is **irrelevant.** It talks about the actions Lady Wintergreen has taken.

(B) says that Cordelia was a source of comfort to her mother, but it does not talk about how. Therefore, it is relevant, but the **relationship** with the subject is **not strong** enough.

(D) is again about Cordelia, but the **relationship** to the subject is **not strong**: it does not talk about how Cordelia is comforting her mother by understanding her feelings.

5 Graph Questions: Pattern Hunter

Type 1: Graph Analysis

The first type of question depends more on how well you understand the graph than how well you have understood the passage. Therefore, it would be helpful to focus on the graph rather than the passage for these questions.

> Tip: Graph-Specific Terms to Remember
> - Upward, increase, double, triple: the bars or lines in the graph point upwards
> - Downward, decrease: the bars or lines in the graph point downwards
> - Appreciable change: a noticeable change
> - Skyrocket: dramatic increase
> - Plummet: dramatic decrease
> - Peak: the highest point in the graph

Graph Sample Passages

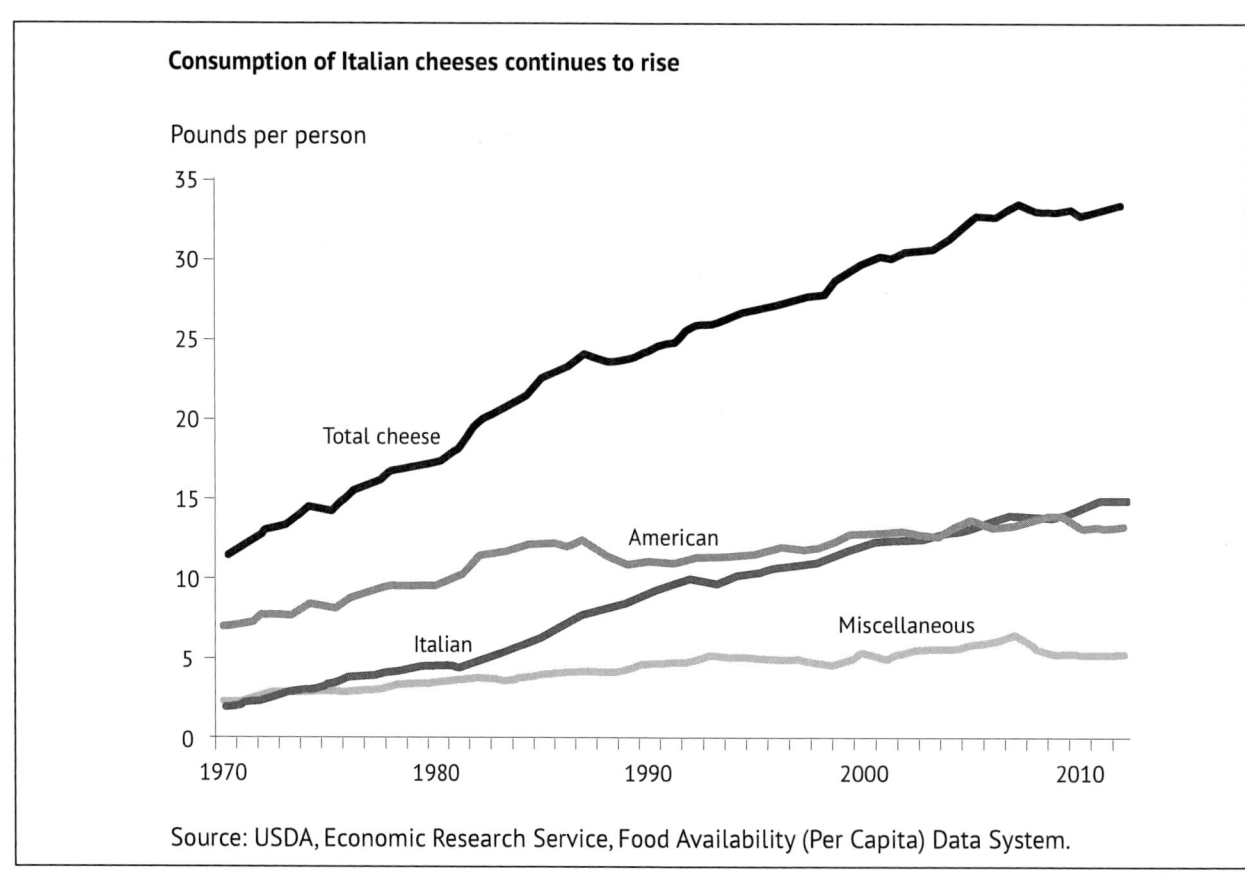

46 | Paul's SAT Reading

> 1. According to the graph, which statement is true about the amount of consumed cheese from 1970 to 2010?
>   (A) The cheese consumption of miscellaneous people from 1970-1990 was wildly out of proportion to the amount consumed from 1990-2010.
>   (B) The amount of cheese consumed by the average Italian was initially greater than the amount consumed by the average American.
>   (C) The amount of total cheese consumption peaked in 2000.
>   (D) The amount of cheese consumed by the average Italian has risen steadily from 1970, surpassing the amount consumed by the average American around 2005.

Q1 Answer Key : (D)

First, Read the title of the graph and the small explanation.
Title: Consumption of Cheese, 1970-2010
So, the main subject of this graph is the amount of cheese being consumed.

Second, Look at the X-axis and Y-axis.
Y-axis: The pounds of cheese that one person eats
X-axis: 1970-2010
Third, Where is the graph heading?
All of the lines in the graph are heading upwards, showing an INCREASE in the amount of cheese consumed.

Now let's take a look at the answer choices for one that is TRUE.

(A) is wrong, because the amount of cheese consumption by miscellaneous people doesn't change much from 1970-2010. There's only a slight rise.
(B) The amount of cheese consumed by the average Italian was not initially greater than the amount consumed by the average American. In fact, the average Italian ate less cheese than the average American at first.
(C) "Peaked" means that the amount eaten should be highest in 2000, but it just keeps rising after that, so this is also wrong.

Therefore, (D) is the correct answer.

Type 2

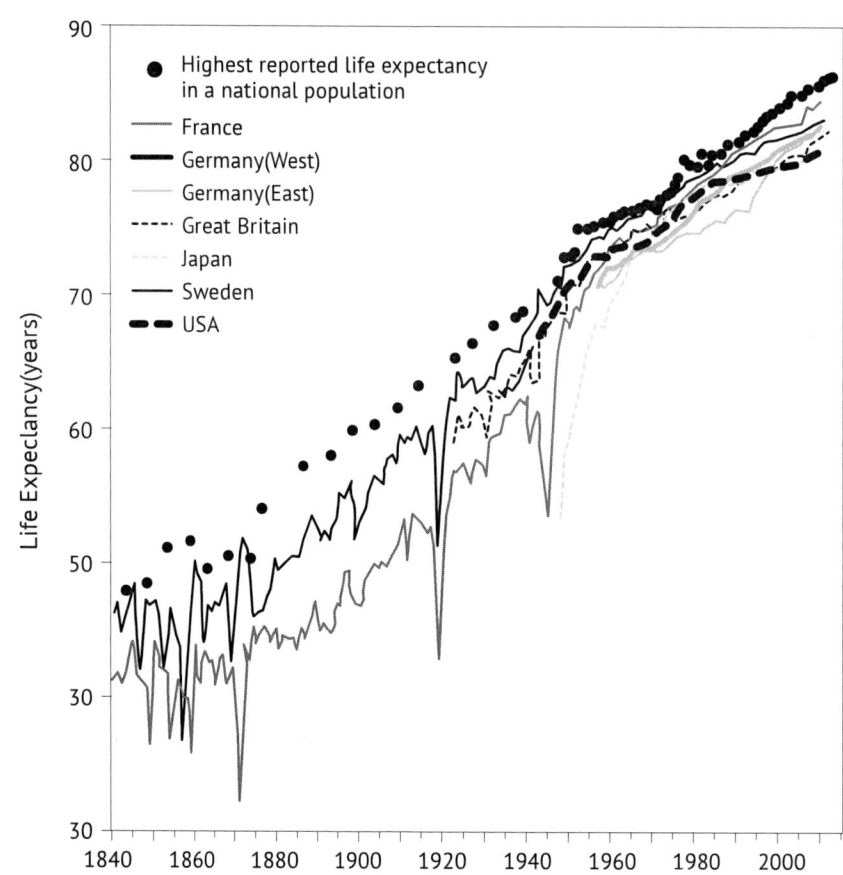

Although literature and language is full of expressions about the brevity of human life, technology has brought us the mixed blessing of extending our lives by several decades. If you were born anywhere between the Paleolithic times to the Middle Ages, dying in your twenties was a common occurrence, and surviving up to forty was seen as fortunate. With the advent of the 19th century, however, life expectancy at birth has increased every year. Life
5 expectancy leaped to even longer numbers by the end of the 20th century. From a life expectancy of 50 in 1900, we have advanced to a life expectancy of over 70 in the majority of countries. With countries like Japan and Sweden vying for the top, life expectancies have been escalating steadily for the past several decades and show no sign of abating.

This projection has been supported by a stream of steady research - from the Buck Institute, where they have quadrupled the lifespan of lab worms, to the California Life Company, where Google's vast resources are used to study
10 longevity. As fertility rates decrease and causes of death change from contagious diseases to noncommunicable ones, the elderly population is sure to swell. However, the people who had searched so eagerly for a modern-day alchemist's stone are not so certain if this is a cheerful future to anticipate. Eking out another decade in disease and discomfort sounds like an inelegant option for many; and the younger generation is wary of being burdened by costly healthcare services and rapidly growing welfare services. If the elderly live longer and keep voting for measures that will put a
15 financial burden on us, goes the argument, more urgent areas in society could go without assistance.

1. Which of the following discussed in the passage is represented by the graph?
(A) Lines 2-4 ("If ... fortunate")
(B) Lines 6-7 ("With ... abating")
(C) Lines 8-10 ("This ... longevity")
(D) Lines 10-11 ("As ... swell")

Q1 Answer Key : (B)

Remember, look for *keywords* in the lines that are similar to what is shown in the graph!

The graph is showing how **life expectancies** in many different countries have **increased over 1840-2000**. Now, let's look for answer choices that convey a similar meaning.

(A) is a small detail about the life expectancy from the Paleolithic Age to the Middle Ages, not from 1840 to 2000. Therefore, eliminate!

(C) is about the various research and studies conducted about longevity. It does not have much relevance to the graph.

(D) is about how elderly people will increase in number, and why. It is not about increased life expectancy.

(B), however, contains many important keywords that match with the graph, including "life expectancy," "past few decades," and accurately points out that the graph is increasing.

Therefore, (B) is the correct answer.

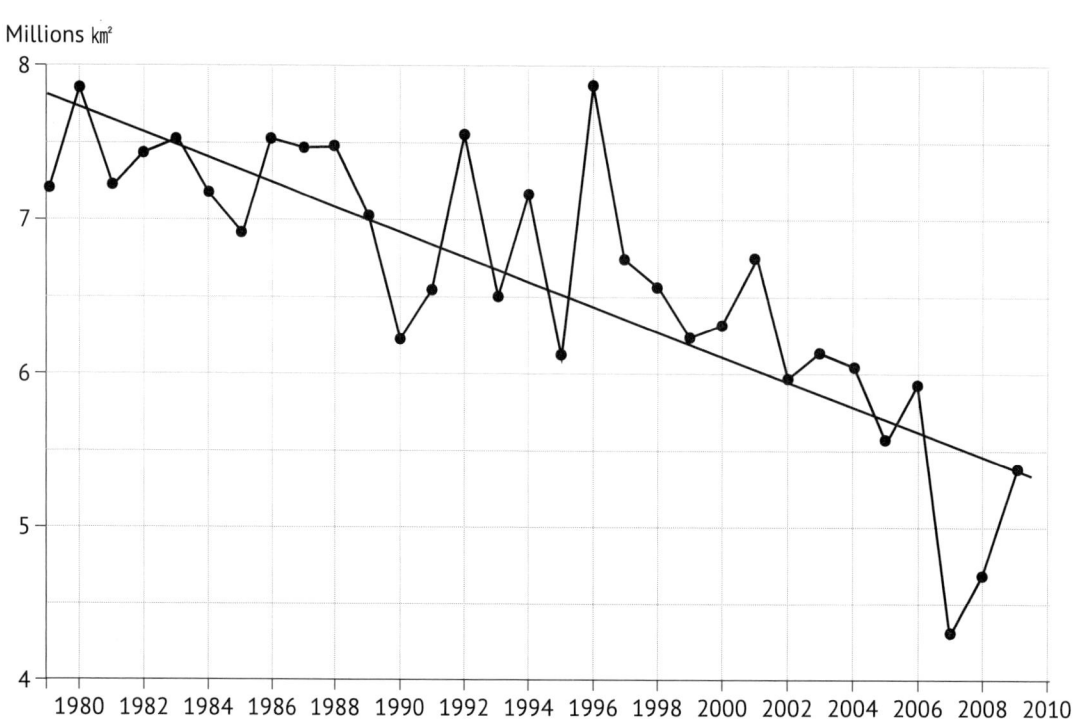

The ebb and flow of Arctic ice is nothing new: waters rise, plankton bloom, wildlife feed, and then the ice thickens again, providing a marble-white foundation on which this exotic continent is anchored. However, the Arctic has not escaped the ravages of global warming, and the firmly layered ice is melting away, taking with them whole ecosystems. A common reference to this phenomenon is the mournful polar bear clutching onto the last ice floe, but
5 it affects more than polar bears: it is causing a decline of biodiversity, a loss of habitats, ocean stratification, and a dangerous rise in ocean temperatures.

The last symptom is all the more grave because, in a system of positive feedback, it triggers a vicious cycle. As ice reflects sunlight, while dark water absorbs it, less ice means warmer waters, and warmer waters means even less ice, and on and on, gnawing away not only at the thin annual ice but also, more alarmingly, multilayer ice that dates back
10 to nine years and is known to be very stable. Despite the annual flux of ice melting and reforming, studies show a persistent, steady decline that bodes no good for the 21st century.

2. Which of the following lines best represent what is shown in the graph?
(A) Line 1-2 ("The ... anchored")
(B) Line 4-6 ("A ... temperatures")
(C) Line 7 ("The ... cycle")
(D) Lines 10-11 ("Despite ... century")

Q2 Answer Key : (D)

Let's look at the graph first. What is the *subject* of the graph?

It shows how much ice there is in the Arctic. While it keeps going up and down (as is natural, since the passage mentions that ice increases and decreases every year depending on the season), there is a clear overall trend of going down.

Therefore, we know that the subject of this graph is:

The **decline of Arctic ice**, although it usually melts and reforms by itself.

(A) talks about the ebb and flow of Arctic ice, but mentions nothing about its decline.

(B) talks about polar bears and other *consequences* of Arctic ice decline, but doesn't say much about the decline itself.

The subject of (C) is rising ocean temperatures and their effects, not Arctic ice decline.

Therefore, the answer is (D).

6. Time Management: MCSx2, Pick One, Move On

Given enough time, almost anyone would be able to figure out the correct answer to the questions on the Redesigned SAT Reading Section. They are not extremely difficult, and unlike the old SAT, they do not often try to trick you with difficult word play or words with double meanings, and they do not penalize you for incorrect answers. Almost anyone with an hour to read and think could score well on the Reading.

The problem is, no matter who you are, or what level your reading ability is, there *will* be questions that you are unable to answer quickly. In order to maximize your score, you need to be as good at admitting ignorance on these questions as you are at answering the questions you can figure out.

Here's how we do it:

Total time for Entire Reading Section: **65 minutes**

*Total time **per passage** (including marking answers):* 65/5 = **about 13 minutes**

*Total time for **reading** each passage:* less than **4 minutes**

*Total time for answering **all** 10-11 questions:* less than **10 minutes**

After you have spent your 3-4 minutes reading a passage, quickly review *all* the questions for that passage.

Notice that the time limits above don't add up directly to 65 minutes. This is because some passages are longer, and some are shorter, some are easier and some are harder. It is up to you to figure out which passages you should devote the most time to. To decide which passages to focus on, decide which ones you stand the best chance of answering the most correct questions on. In order to figure out which questions to focus on, you need to do a survey of all the questions to ensure that you don't run out of time and accidentally skip a question that you could have answered correctly. Here is how to manage that process.

First, for every passage **except for literary passages, scan them, don't read them**. The questions are easy enough that it isn't necessary to read all of the passages thoroughly. Read the first paragraph, the first and last sentences of each paragraph, then the last paragraph. Once this is done, **start with the questions**. If you can quickly answer a question, do so and **mark it with an O**. Otherwise, mark difficult questions with an X and move on. For the remainder of your 8-10 minutes, always go to the **next easiest X question** until you are out of questions or you are out of time. If much more than 13 minutes have passed, **move on to the next passage, no matter what.**

If you are able to read and address the questions of all five passages with time to spare, **only then** should you return to previous passages to address unanswered X questions. If you have any unanswered questions as time runs out, make your best guess or fill in the blank randomly. Wrong answers are not penalized, so this can only help you.

While you are studying practice passages, **make sure to mark every question with an O or X.** Keep track of how many O questions you get right and how many X questions you get wrong. Your target should be to get all of your O questions right. The closer you are to this goal, the more confident you can be in how you spend your time during the test.

Be brutal and honest with yourself. Admit it when you do not know the answer. Time spent on an unanswerable question is time you *could have* spent on an answerable one. Remember, it isn't necessarily about answering all the questions, **it is about marking all the ones you *can* answer.**

What follows in this instruction booklet is intended only to help you better understand the passages as you read them. Only follow the instructions that do not slow you down. If you find something that is too difficult or causes you to answer fewer questions, then do not do it. The most important thing to do is to make sure you are answering all the questions you can answer.

Answer Explanations for Practice Test X
Process of Elimination Code (see Chapter 1 for explanation)

1. NM - Not Mentioned - There is no mention of this topic in the passage
2. NI - Not the Issue - There is a mention of this topic in the passage, but it does not answer the question, or is the wrong focus for the question
3. 2Str - Too Strong - This word is too strong to be considered correct
4. 2Gen - Too General - This word is too general to be considered correct for the concepts in the passage
5. 2Spc - Too Specific - This word is too specific to be considered correct for the concepts in the passage
6. Opp - Opposite - This phrase is the opposite of whatever the correct answer is
7. Y - this part of the question is actually correct

4 Practice Tests

Part 1

SAT® Practice Test #1

Reading Test

65 MINUTES, 52 QUESTIONS

Turn to Section 1 of your answer sheet to answer the questions in this section.

DIRECTIONS

Each passage or pair of passages below is followed by a number of questions. After reading each passage or pair, choose the best answer to each question based on what is stated or implied in the passage or passages and in any accompanying graphics (such as a table or graph).

Questions 1-10 are based on the following passage.

This passage is adapted from *Wuthering Heights* by Emily Bronte. Originally published in 1847.

I was superstitious about dreams then, and am still; and Catherine had an unusual gloom in her aspect, that made me dread something from which I might shape a prophecy, and foresee a fearful catastrophe.
[5] She recommenced in a short time.

'If I were in heaven, Nelly, I should be extremely miserable.'

'Because you are not fit to go there,' I answered. 'All sinners would be miserable in heaven.'

[10] 'But it is not for that. I dreamt once that I was there.'

'I tell you I won't hearken to your dreams, Miss Catherine!' I interrupted again.

'This is nothing,' cried she: 'I was only going to [15] say that heaven did not seem to be my home; and I broke my heart with weeping to come back to earth; and the angels were so angry that they flung me out into the middle of the heath on the top of Wuthering Heights; where I woke sobbing for joy. That will do [20] to explain my secret. I've no more business to marry Edgar Linton than I have to be in heaven; and if the wicked man in there had not brought Heathcliff so low, I shouldn't have thought of it. It would degrade me to marry Heathcliff now; so he shall never know [25] how I love him: and that, not because he's handsome, Nelly, but because he's more myself than I am. Whatever our souls are made of, his and mine are the same; and Linton's is as different as a moonbeam from lightning, or frost from fire.'

[30] 'Joseph is here,' I answered, sighing upon catching the opportune roll of his cartwheels up the road; 'and Heathcliff will come in with him.'

'Oh, he couldn't overhear me at the door!' said she. 'I want to cheat my uncomfortable conscience, [35] and be convinced that Heathcliff has no notion of these things. He has not, has he? He does not know what being in love is!'

'I see no reason that he should not know, as well as you,' I returned; 'and if you are his choice, he'll [40] be the most unfortunate creature that ever was born! Have you considered how you'll bear the separation, and how he'll bear to be quite deserted in the world?'

'He quite deserted! We separated!' she exclaimed, [45] with an accent of indignation. 'Who is to separate us, pray? Not as long as I live, Ellen: for no mortal creature. Every Linton on the face of the earth might melt into nothing before I could consent to forsake Heathcliff. Oh, that's not what I intend—that's not [50] what I mean! I shouldn't be Mrs. Linton were such a price demanded! He'll be as much to me as he has been all his lifetime. Edgar must shake off his antipathy, and tolerate him, at least. He will, when he learns my true feelings towards him. Nelly, I see [55] now you think me a selfish wretch; but did it never strike you that if Heathcliff and I married, we should be beggars? Whereas, if I marry Linton I can aid Heathcliff to rise, and place him out of my brother's power.'

'With your husband's money, Miss Catherine?' I asked. 'You'll find him not so pliable as you calculate upon: and, though I'm hardly a judge, I think that's the worst motive you've given yet for being the wife of young Linton.'

'It is not,' retorted she; 'it is the best! The others were the satisfaction of my whims: and for Edgar's sake, too, to satisfy him. This is for the sake of one who comprehends in his person my feelings to Edgar and myself. I cannot express it; but surely you and everybody have a notion that there is or should be an existence of yours beyond you. What were the use of my creation, if I were entirely contained here? My great miseries in this world have been Heathcliff's miseries, and I watched and felt each from the beginning: my great thought in living is himself. If all else perished, and he remained, I should still continue to be; and if all else remained, and he were annihilated, the universe would turn to a mighty stranger: I should not seem a part of it.—My love for Linton is like the foliage in the woods: time will change it, I'm well aware, as winter changes the trees. Nelly, I am Heathcliff! He's always, always in my mind: not as a pleasure, any more than I am always a pleasure to myself, but as my own being. So don't—'

She paused, and hid her face in the folds of my gown; but I jerked it forcibly away. I was out of patience with her folly!

1

Which choice best describes what happens in the passage?
A) One character criticizes another for pursuing a dishonorable plan.
B) One character reveals the true motivations behind a decision.
C) One character resigns herself to the will of another.
D) One character confronts another's intrusion on her privacy.

2

Which choice best describes the structural development of the passage?
A) A detailed retelling of a dramatic encounter
B) An emotional disclosure of private feelings
C) A strategic analysis of risks and benefits
D) A casual conversation between close friends

3

As used in line 2, "aspect" most nearly means
A) view.
B) outlook.
C) character.
D) appearance.

4

It is implied that Catherine is most concerned about which of the following outcomes?
A) That Edgar mistakes her kindness for love
B) That Edgar withdraws his offer of marriage
C) That Heathcliff considers her marriage an act of desertion
D) That Heathcliff underestimates the sincerity of her promises

5

Which choice provides the best evidence for the answer to the previous question?
A) Lines 38-40 ("I...born")
B) Lines 47-50 ("Every...mean")
C) Lines 57-59 ("whereas...power")
D) Lines 65-67 ("The others...him")

6

Throughout the passage, the narrator treats Catherine with
A) respect but not true affection.
B) leniency but not overindulgence.
C) disapproval but not outright hostility.
D) humor but not blatant disregard.

7

The primary purpose of the lines 19-26("That...I am") is to
A) relay a message.
B) make a comparison.
C) correct a misunderstanding.
D) analyze a decision.

8

As used in line 35, "notion" most nearly means
A) awareness.
B) motivation.
C) illusion.
D) belief.

9

Why does Catherine say in line 75 that her "great thought in living" is Heathcliff?
A) She fears that her love for Edgar will fade with time.
B) She feels she can offer him a new chance at life.
C) She knows her feelings for Heathcliff are more significant than her sense of self.
D) She worries that Heathcliff will never forgive her.

10

Which choice provides the best evidence for the answer to the previous question?
A) Lines 67-69 ("This...myself")
B) Lines 69-71 ("But surely...you")
C) Lines 79-82 ("My...trees")
D) Lines 82-84 ("He's...being")

Questions 11-21 are based on the following passage and supplementary material.

This passage is adapted from "Is It Art or Knowledge? Deconstructing Australian Aboriginal Creative Making" by Elizabeth Cameron, 2015.

Australian Aboriginal symbols are visual forms of knowledge that express cultural intellect within a sense of place and spiritual space. There are more than 350
Line different Aboriginal Nations in Australia, and each
5 group has its own creative expressions of knowledge with unique designs, symbols, techniques, and mediums. These symbolic markings, lines and patterns remain the intellectual property of each Nation, but are nonetheless all bound within customary laws associated
10 to traditional creation stories, known collectively as "The Dreaming." Aboriginal creativity has little concept of aesthetic value, but instead focuses on displaying a specific interpretation of the The Dreaming and its unique meaning to each Nation.

15 The Dharug Nation, located around the northern Sydney area of New South Wales, refers to its traditional ritualized customary lore surrounding The Dreaming as "Gunyalungalung." The symbols of Gunyalungalung are permanently located within the
20 Dharug environment on open rock surfaces, caves and tree carvings. While some symbols are manmade, others are said to be made by ancestral beings from the time of Creation and contain deeply sacred story lines. Therefore, this creative imagery engraved or
25 painted on rock surfaces is more than simply art, but a form of conscious narrative that emphasizes deep insight and connection to the land and the history of the Nation. It is said that this depth of connection allows a free flow of meaning between the external
30 objective reality of the physical environment and the subjective internal spiritual world.

Thus, classification of these works into a Western interpretation of "art" undervalues thousands of years of generational knowledge systems. An alternative
35 understanding is required to appreciate how the Aboriginal cultural framework illustrates knowledge and therefore has little relevance to aesthetic pleasure in viewing, or "acquirement" as a sense of ownership. Instead, Aboriginal "art" reflects vital information about
40 existence itself. For example, many symbols located around rock formations contain animal symbols that inform bypassers of what foods may be located within the area, as well as the connection of those animals to stories stretching back thousands of years.

45 In understanding cultural differences within visual expressions it is necessary to reflect on the wisdom and knowledge built over generations. This can be difficult for non-Indigenous cultures, who tend to approach imagery from an external perspective, rather
50 than by considering the deep metaphorical elements that lie beneath what is merely "seen". Perhaps there is also occasionally a sense of prejudgment. Many non-Indigenous people see these symbols as mere forms of communication, or worse, from
55 preconceptions of primitiveness.

Utilizing visual content, Dharug storytelling ensures that cultural messages are imprinted upon the next generation. Worldviews are expressed through comprehensive dialects within a collective intellectual
60 space. What might appear primitive is instead the result of understanding that simple visual imagery is more easily stored in memory, and is thus intentional. The additional use of repetitive patterning assists in memory recall, by generating rhythmical energies. The
65 circle, for example, when used in a repetitive manner illustrates cyclical and harmonious space that ensures both conscious and unconscious responses are locked into the memory.

"Self" within the Dharug concept is not a
70 consideration, since social involvement is a priority. Elaborating further, self is considered only an aspect of knowledge, whereas the collective has ultimate knowledge. The patterning of the environment forms a conscious reminder of our valuable relationships to all
75 living things.

A sense of cultural place within the Dharug conception relates to "feelings associated with identity" with a focus on community belonging. It is a place that is central to Dharug philosophical life purpose, as
80 the concept of land is not connected to self-ownership—rather, it is a state of internal wealth where customary obligations in caring for "the nation" are fulfilled and maintained. Spiritual space provides a sense of purpose to living, and appears through
85 dreams, visions and ancestral guidance. Therefore, "cultural" place and "spiritual" space are connected to philosophical understanding within the Dharug Gunyalungalung.

Examples of Prehistoric Art
Containing Specific Symbols
(Percentage of Sites by Continent)

	Circle	Cross	Cross hatch	Hand form	Snake form	Dots	Angles
Australia	20%	60%	80%	10%	30%	100%	70%
Africa	0%	40%	55%	20%	70%	75%	60%
North America	80%	0%	0%	70%	40%	30%	25%
South America	65%	15%	10%	0%	30%	90%	50%
Asia	90%	70%	60%	0%	0%	20%	90%
Europe	60%	100%	95%	30%	5%	0%	50%

11

The author most likely uses the examples listed in lines 3-7 ("There...mediums") in order to emphasize the
A) difficulty an outsider might have in learning Aboriginal language.
B) complexity involved in comprehending Aboriginal culture.
C) wide variety of possible Aboriginal cultural manifestations.
D) recent decline in the number of Aboriginal tribes.

12

As used in line 39, "vital" most nearly means
A) urgent.
B) energetic.
C) important.
D) forceful.

13

The author indicates that the "art" of Aboriginal nations
A) provides a point of reference between previously hostile tribes.
B) serves as a link between physical and mental realities.
C) brightens the otherwise empty and unforgiving Australian Outback.
D) exceeds even the many successes of Western artistic traditions.

14

Which choice provides the best evidence for the answer to the previous question?
A) Lines 7-11 ("These...Dreaming")
B) Lines 18-21 ("The symbols...tree carvings")
C) Lines 28-31 ("It...world")
D) Lines 32-34 ("Thus...systems")

15

The "350 different Aboriginal Nations" mentioned in the first paragraph (lines 3-7) would likely describe "Gunyalungalung" as
A) surprising.
B) unremarkable.
C) problematic.
D) characteristic.

16

The passage indicates that the judgments made by "non-Indigenous" people in line 53 are best characterized as
A) well-intentioned.
B) justified.
C) limited.
D) impossible.

17

Which choice provides the best evidence for the answer to the previous question?
A) Lines 40-44 ("For example...years")
B) Lines 45-47 ("In understanding...generations")
C) Lines 58-60 ("Worldviews...space")
D) Lines 60-62 ("What might...intentional")

18

As used in line 72, "collective" most nearly means
A) communal.
B) composite.
C) augmented.
D) concentrated.

19

The authors discuss the Dharug conception of self (lines 69-75) in order to
A) clarify a misconception.
B) disprove a claim.
C) challenge a widely-held belief.
D) establish a contrast.

20

Which of the following relationships most closely resembles the relationship described in the final paragraph of the passage?
A) A key and a lock
B) A puzzle piece and a completed puzzle
C) A needle and thread
D) A book and its table of contents

21

The chart following the passage provides evidence that compared to the other regions in the chart, prehistoric Australians used
A) a wider variety of symbols.
B) more dots and angles in their religious ceremonies.
C) far fewer hand form symbols.
D) only those symbols which could be permanently etched into the environment.

Questions 22-31 are based on the following passage and supplementary material.

This passage is adapted from "Impacts of Beech Bark Disease and Climate Change on American Beech" by Christopher Alexander Stephanson and Natalie Ribarik Coe, 2017.

American beech (*Fagus grandifolia*) is a dominant component of forest tree cover over a large portion of eastern North America and this deciduous, mast-bearing
[Line 5] tree species plays a key role in these forest ecosystems. Beech bark disease (BBD) is a scale insect-fungus complex that has caused the decline and death of afflicted beech trees. Described as "an old disease in a new place," BBD in American beech is the result of an inadvertent introduction of a European
[10] pathogen to North America. Resistance to BBD is contingent on the beech scale. Beech scale attack predisposes the tree to infection by harmful fungi. The infection rates of beech have proved to be devastating in the United States; an 80-90% rate of infection
[15] within a group of trees is not unusual. Today, scale-free trees have been reported within only 1% to 3% of measured areas, with estimates ranging from 80-95% of overall infestation for all North American beech, with over 50% dead or dying from the disease.
[20] Additionally, overall beech health will be directly impacted by climate change, given the expected fluctuations in precipitation leading to both drought periods and flooding.

Given the huge geographical extent of American
[25] beech, the effects of global climate change on BBD progression is expected to be diverse in some respects. The scale can overwinter quite efficiently in even bitterly cold conditions. Warmer winters may favor the survival and growth of both the scale and fungus. The
[30] scale is often hidden under the leaves at the bottom of the tree and will begin to attack at the tree base. Unless the litter is removed and the bark at the tree base is carefully examined, a tree may only appear to be resistant to BBD. Regardless of its first point of
[35] attack, the disease can cover the full perimeter of the trunk relatively quickly. A highly susceptible tree will go from little to no infection to dead from BBD in less than ten years. There is no doubt that climate change favors propagation of the pathogens responsible
[40] for BBD, and although the beech range is expected to expand north, if temperatures continue to rise, this adaptive advantage for combating the pathogens is lost.

Droughts and elevated summer temperatures have already been attributed to global climate change, so
[45] these circumstances are to be expected for groups of North American beech. Drought conditions will decrease nitrogen soil uptake capacity of beech which will in turn reduce growth. Curiously, should bark nitrogen levels be lower in certain American beech
[50] populations, this may inadvertently protect them from host invasion in that the scale prefer old growth to secondary growth trees, presumably because of higher bark nitrogen levels. This protection will be only short term and relative to the natural range of
[55] nitrogen bark concentration in a given area of trees, however. Lower bark nitrogen may benefit a group of trees overall, but will not prevent infestation.

Ideal management now would include the introduction of disease-resistant beech into more
[60] northern reaches of the current range to help speed the migration and increase the likelihood that seed will be dispersed at a rate demanded by elevated temperature and drought conditions. As beech move north, it may take some time for mature and larger
[65] trees to become established and the scale infestation may lag behind significantly. Perhaps before this potential pathogen-host matchup occurs, the ability to screen American beech trees for resistance, or purposefully plant resistant trees may halt the disease
[70] progression and allow prevention and control of further infestation. Although American beech does not garner the interest of European beech for commercial harvesting, it is important that to learn from what has been done in Europe when considering management
[75] of American beech. Studies in European beech have shown a positive response in beech to thinning in order to reduce competition. It is speculated that thinning can counteract the impacts of increased temperature as beech are particular sensitive to water
[80] availability.

The continuing progression of BBD, is poised to greatly diminish the existence of beech-dominated forests. The impacts of climate change will also not brighten the future for BBD-infected forests from the
[85] perspective of the

American beech. The expected changes in temperature and precipitation favor the exotic, invasive pathogens, not the beech. As beech have been selected for
90 BBD-resistance in the microevolution of the past century, climate change will yet again provide additional pressures and selection, testing the ability of the species to survive. However, with concrete restoration efforts currently underway, we may be able
95 to find a human solution to a human-caused problem.

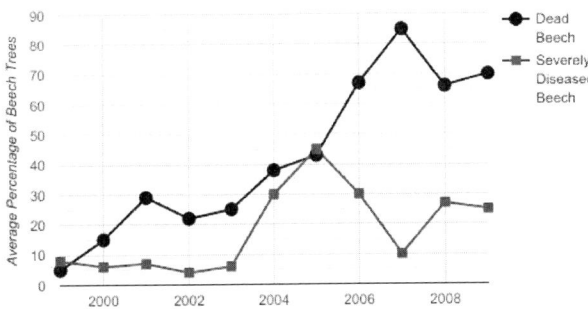

22

The author uses the word "predisposes" in line 12 to indicate that
A) beech scale attacks determine overall infection rates in North American beech ranges.
B) fungi increase average rates of death in American beech trees.
C) resistance to BBD is highly unlikely given the strength of harmful fungi.
D) beech trees with scale infestation are more susceptible to being contaminated by harmful fungi.

23

A student claims that scale insect-fungus are only viable in temperate climates. Which of the following statements in the passage contradicts the student's claim?
A) Lines 27-28 ("The scale...conditions")
B) Lines 28-29 ("Warmer winters...fungus")
C) Lines 34-36 ("Regardless of...quickly")
D) Lines 38-42 ("There is...lost")

24

The author's main purpose of including information about the expected outcomes of climate change on beech bark disease is to
A) confirm the relationship between milder winters and decreased scale and fungus.
B) establish that geography is not guaranteed to aid existing beech populations.
C) present an alternate hypothesis about the effects of low temperatures on scale infection.
D) provide support for the author's claim about the adaptive benefits of beech migration.

25

In the third paragraph (lines 43-57), what does the author claim to be a feature of interest?
A) The link between droughts and beech tree deaths
B) The advantages of old growth trees
C) The unexpected benefits of lower nitrogen in bark
D) The impact of drought on chemical compositions

26

Based on the passage, the author's statement, "Studies in European beech have shown a positive response of beech to thinning to reduce competition" (lines 75-77) implies that the author believes
A) European beech management is more advanced than management of American beech.
B) reducing beech populations can help lower temperatures.
C) European beech have greater water availability and reduced disease progression.
D) selective removal of American beech can prevent further infestation.

27

The author's use of the words "poised," "invasive," and "testing" in lines 83-92 in the final paragraph functions mainly to
A) establish the persistence of beech bark disease despite resistance efforts.
B) counter the claim that existing beech populations have a chance of survival.
C) emphasize the intensity of the impact of BBD and climate change on beech trees.
D) support the claim that BBD favors foreign over native pathogens.

28

Based on the graph, which choice gives the closest approximations of the highest percentage of dead and severely diseased beech trees from 1999 to 2009?
A) 81 and 66
B) 85 and 45
C) 80 and 55
D) 99 and 10

29

Do the data in the graph support the author's claim that over 50% of all beech trees in North America are currently dead or dying?
A) Yes, because the most recent points of data show that 75-95% of beech are dead.
B) Yes, because over 50% of all beech trees in North America are dead after 2006.
C) No, because less than 50% of beech trees were dead or dying between 1999 and 2004.
D) No, because the number of severely diseased beech trees is similar to the number of dead trees.

30

According to the graph, which of the following years provides evidence in support of the answer to the previous question?
A) 1999-2004
B) 2004-2006
C) 2005-2007
D) 2006-2009

31

Based on the graph, which statement made by the author is most consistent with the data?
A) Lines 36-38 ("A highly...years")
B) Lines 53-56 ("This protection...however")
C) Lines 63-66 ("As beech...significantly")
D) Lines 81-83 ("The...forests")

Questions 32-41 are based on the following passage.

This passage is excerpt from "Text Of President John Kennedy's Rice Stadium Moon Speech" by John F. Kennedy, 1962.

Despite the striking fact that most of the scientists that the world has ever known are alive and working today, despite the fact that this Nation's own scientific manpower is doubling every 12 years in a rate of growth more than three times that of our population as a whole, despite that, the vast stretches of the unknown, unanswered, and unfinished still far outstrip our collective comprehension.

No man can fully grasp how far and how fast we have come, but condense, if you will, the 50,000 years of man's recorded history in a time span of but a half-century. Stated in these terms, we know very little about the first 40 years, except at the end of them advanced man had learned to use the skins of animals to cover themselves. Then about 10 years ago on this timeline, man emerged from his caves to construct other kinds of shelter. Only five years ago did man learn to write and use a cart with wheels. The printing press came only this year, and then less than two months ago, during this whole 50-year span of human history, the steam engine provided a new source of power. Last month electric lights and telephones and automobiles and airplanes became available. Only last week did we develop penicillin and television and nuclear power, and now if America's new spacecraft succeeds in reaching Venus, we will have literally reached the stars just before midnight tonight.

The exploration of space will go ahead, whether we join in it or not, and it is one of the great adventures of all time, and no nation which expects to be the leader of other nations can expect to stay behind in the race for space. Those who came before us made certain that this country rode the first waves of the industrial revolutions, the first waves of modern invention, and the first wave of nuclear power, and this generation does not intend to founder in the backwash of the coming age of space. We mean to be a part of it—we mean to lead it.

Yet the vows of this Nation can only be fulfilled if we in this Nation are first, and, therefore, we intend to be first. In short, our leadership in science and in industry, our hopes for peace and security, our obligations to ourselves as well as others, all require us to make this effort, to solve these mysteries, to solve them for the good of all men, and to become the world's leading space-faring nation. We set sail on this new sea because there is new knowledge to be gained, and new rights to be won, and they must be won and used for the progress of all people. Whether it will become a force for good or ill depends on man, and only if the United States occupies a position of pre-eminence can we help decide whether this new ocean will be a sea of peace or a new terrifying theater of war.

But why, some say, the moon? Why choose this as our goal? And they may well ask why climb the highest mountain? We choose to go to the moon. We choose to go to the moon in this decade and do the other things, not because they are easy, but because they are hard, because that goal will serve to organize and measure the best of our energies and skills, because that challenge is one that we are willing to accept, one we are unwilling to postpone, and one which we intend to win, and the others, too.

To be sure, we are behind, and will be behind for some time. But we do not intend to stay behind, and in this decade, we shall make up and move ahead. The growth of our science and education will be enriched by new knowledge of our universe and environment. Space and related industries are generating new demands in investment and skilled personnel, and this city and this State, and this region, will share greatly in this growth.

Many years ago the great British explorer George Mallory, who was to die on Mount Everest, was asked why did he want to climb it. He said, "Because it is there." Well, space is there, and we're going to climb it, and the moon and the planets are there, and new hopes for knowledge and peace are there.

32

The main purpose of the passage is to
A) highlight the value of space exploration.
B) stress the urgency of an undertaking.
C) emphasize the feasibility of national goals.
D) question the underlying motives for exploring space.

33

The central claim of the passage is that
A) American scientists face an immense challenge in taking the lead in the space race.
B) Americans are willing to take on the most difficult tasks in order to assert dominance over all nations.
C) the American people must unite and use their positions of influence to become the leading nation of the space age.
D) America holds full responsibility for preventing warfare between nations over the race for space.

34

Kennedy uses the word "we" throughout the passage mainly to
A) reinforce the need for immediate action among a group of people.
B) establish a sense of solidarity among a group of people.
C) reflect the familial bond among a group of people.
D) promote the need for bravery among a group of people.

35

In the first paragraph, Kennedy chooses to reframe human history into a half-century in order to
A) illustrate the rapid pace of human scientific development in a relatively brief amount of time.
B) criticize the lack of national development in space science despite various recent technological advancements.
C) promote a mood of inspirational contemplation for a nation scarred by war.
D) honor the legacy of the past and future contributors to technological development.

36

Kennedy indicates that to lead other nations in the space age is
A) required in order to finally earn their respect.
B) rooted in the legacy of America's forefathers.
C) vital for preventing cooperation among America's enemies.
D) dependent upon the generation of new jobs by American industries.

37

Which choice provides the best evidence for the answer to the previous question?
A) Lines 1-8 ("Despite...comprehension")
B) Lines 32-37 ("Those...space")
C) Lines 46-54 ("We set...war")
D) Lines 70-73 ("Space...growth")

38

In the passage, Kennedy characterizes the exploration of the moon as both
A) guaranteed and momentous.
B) disturbing and appealing.
C) daunting and uncompromising.
D) strange and pressing.

39

Which choice provides the best evidence for the answer to the previous question?
A) Lines 28-32 ("The exploration...space")
B) Lines 49-54 ("Whether...war")
C) Lines 57-64 ("We...too")
D) Lines 65-67 ("To...ahead")

40

Which choice most closely captures the meaning of the figurative "backwash" referred to in line 37?
A) Opportunity
B) Aftermath
C) Innovation
D) Flood

41

George Malloy's justification for climbing Mount Everest in lines 74-77 ("Many years ago...there") mainly serves to emphasize how
A) novel the challenge faced by scientists is.
B) pervasive the demand for new knowledge and technology is.
C) ambitious the continued exploration of the unknown is.
D) enjoyable the adventures and discoveries of American explorers are.

Questions 42-52 are based on the following passages.

Passage 1 is adapted from "Influence of Amino Acids, Dietary Protein, and Physical Activity on Muscle Mass Development in Humans" by Kasper Dideriksen, 2013. Passage 2 is adapted from "Pre-Sleep Protein Ingestion to Improve the Skeletal Muscle Adaptive Response to Exercise Training" by Jorn Trommelen and Luc J. C. van Loon, 2016.

Passage 1

Ingestion of protein is crucial for the maintenance of a variety of body functions and the regulation of skeletal muscle mass, which is in turn essential for
Line health and quality of life. Due to its large volume
5 relative to the rest of the body, skeletal muscle is the primary site for nutrient use and energy consumption in the body and also plays an essential role in weight regulation. Furthermore, skeletal muscle is responsible for a huge proportion of the storage of amino acids
10 (AA), which are crucial for making acute phase proteins which fight against critical illnesses or heal wounds following severe trauma. Limiting the loss of skeletal muscle mass during periods of illness or injury is necessary for decreasing patient morbidity and
15 increasing recovery outcome.

Recent research has begun to reveal the relationship between protein intake and its resulting stimulation of muscle protein synthesis (anabolism). A quantitative limitation exists as to how much muscle protein the
20 body can synthesize in response to protein intake. Ingestion of excess protein exerts an unwanted load on the body and therefore it is important to find the least amount of protein required to provide maximal growth stimulus. This quantitative limitation, a phenomenon
25 termed the "muscle full" concept, can be modulated by physical activity, in that muscle inactivity narrows the limitations while muscle activity expands them. For example, a greater protein requirement has been reported in bodybuilders and endurance trained athletes
30 as compared to sedentary young men.

Studies have shown that the speed of anabolic response depends on the physical and chemical qualities of whatever protein is ingested, with some reacting more quickly than others. Both "slow" and
35 "fast" proteins have inherent advantages and their specific uses are dependent on the daily life situations in which they are ingested. The effect of protein intake on muscle protein accretion can further be stimulated by prior exercise training. In the ageing
40 population, physical training may counteract the development of "anabolic resistance" and restore the beneficial effect of protein feeding.

Passage 2

45 Protein ingestion following resistance-type exercise stimulates muscle protein synthesis rates, and enhances the skeletal muscle adaptive response to prolonged resistance-type exercise training. As the adaptive response to a single bout of resistance exercise extends well beyond the first couple of hours of post-exercise recovery, research has begun to
50 investigate the impact of the timing and distribution of protein ingestion during more prolonged recovery periods. As overnight sleep is typically the longest post-absorptive period during the day, studies have recently introduced the concept of protein ingestion
55 prior to sleep as a means to augment post-exercise overnight muscle protein synthesis.

A single session of exercise stimulates muscle protein synthesis rates, and to a lesser extent, muscle protein breakdown rates. However, the muscle protein
60 net balance will remain negative if food is not eaten. Protein ingestion stimulates muscle protein synthesis and inhibits muscle protein breakdown rates, resulting in net muscle protein accretion during the most active stages of post-exercise recovery. Therefore,
65 post-exercise protein ingestion is widely applied as a strategy to augment post-exercise muscle protein synthesis rates and, as such, to aid in the growth of skeletal muscle in response to exercise training. Various factors have been identified which can
70 modulate the post-exercise muscle protein synthetic response to exercise including the amount, type, timing, and distribution of protein ingestion.

Besides the amount and type of ingested protein, the timing and distribution of protein ingestion
75 throughout the day can modulate post-exercise muscle protein synthesis rates. Overnight sleep has emerged as a novel window of opportunity to modulate muscle protein metabolism. Recent work has shown that overnight muscle protein synthesis rates are restricted
80 by the level of amino acid availability. Protein ingested immediately prior to sleep is effectively digested and absorbed, and thereby increases amino acid availability during overnight sleep. Greater amino acid availability during sleep stimulates muscle protein
85 synthesis rates and improves whole-body protein net balance during overnight recovery. Furthermore, prior exercise allows more of the pre-sleep protein-derived amino acids to be utilized for muscle protein synthesis during sleep.
90

Resistance-type exercise performed during the day
augments the overnight muscle protein synthetic response to pre-sleep protein ingestion and allows more of the protein-derived amino acids to be used as precursors for muscle protein synthesis. When applied during a prolonged period of resistance-type exercise training, protein supplementation prior to sleep can be used effectively to further increase gains in muscle mass and strength. In short, pre-sleep protein ingestion represents an effective dietary strategy to improve overnight muscle protein synthesis, thereby improving the skeletal muscle adaptive response to exercise training.

42

In lines 9-12, the author of Passage 1 mentions amino acids mainly to
A) provide evidence of improved recovery outcomes.
B) bring attention to their role in regulating weight.
C) emphasize the advantages of increased protein ingestion.
D) highlight the importance of skeletal muscle mass.

43

The author of Passage 1 indicates that increased protein intake could have which effect?
A) It could affect resting metabolic rate.
B) It could cause undue strain on the body.
C) It could promote further anabolic resistance.
D) It could impair muscle protein anabolism in the elderly.

44

Which choice provides the best evidence for the answer to the previous question?
A) Lines 1-4 ("Ingestion...quality")
B) Lines 12-15 ("Limiting...outcome")
C) Lines 18-20 ("A quantitative...intake")
D) Lines 21-24 ("Ingestion...stimulus")

45

As used in line 30, "sedentary" most nearly means
A) subdued.
B) inert.
C) inactive.
D) apathetic.

46

What function does the discussion of the "muscle full" concept in lines 24-30 serve in Passage 1?
A) It provides an alternative solution to a question mentioned in the previous paragraph.
B) It offers an example that supports a claim made in the previous paragraph.
C) It examines the limits of a phenomenon discussed in the previous paragraph.
D) It continues an extended metaphor that begins in the previous paragraph.

47

The central claim of Passage 2 is that pre-sleep protein ingestion has strong potential because
A) it can enhance post-exercise overnight muscle protein synthesis.
B) it alone is effective in stimulating overnight muscle reconditioning.
C) ingestion rates are dependent on the level of amino acid availability.
D) it is the most commercially viable solution available.

48

As used in line 47, "bout" most nearly means
A) contest.
B) encounter.
C) match.
D) session.

49

Which statement best captures the relationship between the passages?
A) Passage 2 disproves the central claim made in Passage 1.
B) Passage 2 provides a specific example of a phenomenon described in Passage 1.
C) Passage 2 argues against the plausibility of the approach proposed in Passage 1.
D) Passage 2 expresses doubt about a proposal made in Passage 1.

50

The author of Passage 2 would most likely respond to the discussion of "slow" and "fast" proteins in lines 40-43, Passage 1, by claiming that
A) "fast" proteins can yield greater benefits than "slow" proteins.
B) overnight sleep is the most efficient means to modulate muscle protein synthesis rates.
C) their usefulness is directly dependent on the frequency of ingestion.
D) they can modulate the rate of post-exercise muscle protein synthesis.

51

Which choice provides the best evidence for the answer to the previous question?
A) Lines 57-59 ("A single...rates")
B) Lines 65-68 ("Therefore...training")
C) Lines 69-72 ("Various...ingestion")
D) Lines 76-78 ("Overnight...metabolism")

52

Which point about amino acids is implicit in Passage 1 and explicit in Passage 2?
A) They will increase in number as they are digested and absorbed.
B) They are likely to stimulate overnight muscle growth.
C) They can restrict overnight muscle protein synthesis rates.
D) They are best utilized when ingested in large quantities.

STOP

If you finish before time is called, you may check your work on this section only.
Do not turn to any other section.

Part 1

Practice Test 1:
Answer Key and Explanations

Reading Test 1 Answer Key

Reading Test 1	
Question	Answer
1	B
2	B
3	D
4	C
5	B
6	C
7	D
8	A
9	C
10	D
11	C
12	C
13	B
14	C
15	D
16	C
17	D
18	A
19	D
20	B
21	A
22	D
23	A
24	B
25	C
26	D

Reading Test 1	
Question	Answer
27	C
28	B
29	B
30	D
31	D
32	B
33	C
34	B
35	A
36	B
37	B
38	C
39	C
40	B
41	C
42	D
43	B
44	D
45	C
46	C
47	A
48	D
49	B
50	D
51	C
52	B

*For self-scoring assessment tables, please turn to page 189.

Passage 1

1

A) Y-NI. Although Nelly certainly does criticize Catherine, this is not the primary focus of the passage. The passage deals more with understanding Catherine's motivations.

B) **ANSWER: Since the "one character" here is referring to Catherine, and Catherine is the main character, this choice best addresses the question. "Decision" refers to Catherine's plan to marry.**

C) 2spc/NI: "resign" is too specific of a word. If anything, Catherine has a definite, active plan in place, so resign is inappropriate.

D) 2spc/NI: "intrusion on her privacy" are the danger words. This is unsubstantiated in the text.

2

A) NM: "dramatic encounter" are the danger words, and there is no dramatic encounter that is discusseD. "Detailed" is potentially NM as well.

B) **ANSWER: "disclosure" is the keyword, as well as "emotional" and "private." Since all of these are substantiated, this answer works best.**

C) NM/2spc/NI: "analysis" and "risks and benefits" lends more towards a science passage, and are inappropriate in this context.

D) Y-NI: "casual" is the danger word. Since the content of discussion is quite heavy, casual is inappropriate. "Close friends" is problematic as well, given the fact that Catherine is addressed as "Miss."

3

A) 2spc: "View" does not fit in this context, since view can mean either scenery or a perspective.

B) Y-2spc: "outlook" is close, but problematic since it means a perspective. We are looking for a more physical word since the sentence (unusual gloom in her aspect) suggests a word like "countenance" or "face" or "look."

C) Y-2spc/NI: same problem as B. "character" is more related to a psychological state, whereas the sentence suggests a physical reaction.

D) **ANSWER: Given that "appearance" is the only physical word, this works best.**

4

A) NM/NI : Catherine has no intentions of being kind or loving.

B) NM: "withdraw" is the danger word, and this possibility is not discussed. The passage assumes that the marriage will happen.

C) **ANSWER: Since Catherine is most concerned about the repercussions for Heathcliff, this is the most appropriate answer choice. This also ties in with the fact that Catherine plans on leveraging her marriage to help Heathcliff. "Desertion" is the danger word, which is substantiated.**

D) Y-NM: "promises" is the danger word, since no promises are explicitly mentioned. There is an underlying, implicit emotional bond, but no explicit promises have been exchanged.

5

A) NI: These lines discuss knowing or not knowing love, not an outcome

B) **ANSWER: These lines show that Catherine has no intention of deserting Heathcliff, thus it works best.**

C) contender, NI: These lines explain Catherine's

logic behind marriage, not a problematic outcome or potential desertion.

D) NI: The focus of this line is on Edgar, so doesn't work with Heathcliff.

6

A) 2spc: "true affection" is difficult to establish. If anything, the passage suggests that the narrator does care for Catherine.

B) contender, 2spc/NM: "leniency" is the danger word, and the passage in lines 8-10 and 41-43 suggest that the narrator is realistic in criticism, not lenient.

C) ANSWER: "outright hostility" are the danger words, and there is no evidence of hostility in the passage. Although there is tension, the narrator never threatens or acts in accordance with "hostile" behavior.

D) NM: "humor" is the danger word, and the passage is far from humorous. Both characters understand that this is a pivotal moment. However, "not blatant disregard" is correct.

7

A) contender, NI: Although the lines indeed do "relay a message," lines 19-26 should be understood within the broader context of the passage due to the nature of the question. As such, it falls a bit short.

B) NI/NM: No comparison is being drawn.

C) NI/NM: there is no misunderstanding

D) ANSWER: Although "analyze" could be a danger word, it makes sense here since the passage focuses on Catherine's decision to marry Edgar despite her doubts.

8

A) ANSWER: Since the later sentences say "he does not know these things," knowing is important (if the student was unable to grasp this fact by the sentence alone).

B) 2spc: "motivation" does not capture what Catherine is trying to convey. The discussion is about feelings, whereas motivation lends more towards calculation and intent.

C) 2gen: "illusion" can be used in a number of ways, and since the word is too general, it is not a good choice.

D) contender-2spc: Although "belief" does share some similarities with "awareness," belief is more directed towards a cogent system of opinions. We are looking more for a word like "understanding," or "realization."

9

A) NI: Although this is mentioned in the passage, she does not "fear" this prospect. Catherine takes this as a given fact.

B) NI: Although this is implied in the passage through a discussion of Catherine's motives, line 75 expresses her love for Heathcliff, not a new chance at life.

C) ANSWER: This answer choice fits best in context, since here Catherine is detailing for powerful emotions for Heathcliff.

D) 2spc: "never" is a danger word, and is difficult to substantiate.

10

A) NI: Edgar is not the focus

B) contender, NI: This answer choice falls short because it fails to discuss Heathcliff.

C) NI: The focus on Edgar is not appropriate here.

D) **ANSWER: This is the best choice since it accurately captures Heathcliff and discusses "being"**

Passage 2

11

A) NI/NM : "language" is the danger word, and is beside the point.

B) contender, NI: although "complexity" somewhat fits (arguable as well, due to the fact that large quantity does not mean difficulty of comprehension), "comprehending" is not the issue. The examples serve to demonstrate variety.

C) **ANSWER: Good fit. The lines contain words such as "unique" that match well with "wide variety."**

D) NM: "recent" is not mentioned in the lines or the passage.

12

A) 2spc: "urgent" has a time element associated with the word, which is unjustified in this case.

B) 2spc: "energetic" is an erroneous synonym for "vital" as used in the context of this sentence. Also, "energetic" suggests physical motion or vigor, which is further out of context.

C) **ANSWER: Given the fact that "vital" is acting as an adjective for "information," "important" fits well.**

D) 2spc/NI: There is no element of coercion, so "forceful" does not make much sense in this context.

13

A) NM: "hostile tribes" is the danger word, and this is not discussed in the passage.

B) **ANSWER: "physical and mental" is a good substitute for the concept of "external reality" and "internal spiritual world" in lines 30-31**

C) NM: The author offers no critique of the Australian Outback, so this answer choice cannot work.

D) NM/NI: Although Western artistic traditions are somewhat discussed, to point of the discussion is to urge different metrics for evaluation, rather than comparing the quality or "successes" of either tradition.

14

A) 2spc/NI: Although these lines mention certain "mental realities" such as intellectual property and symbolism, this answer choice fails to capture "physical realities" in the previous question.

B) NI/NM: The location of the artistic representations are not discussed in any of the answer choices the previous question.

C) **ANSWER: Since "external reality" and "internal spiritual world" fits with "physical and mental realities," this is our answer. It passes the synonym test and answers in the previous question as well.**

D) NI: This answer choice fails to discuss the art of Aboriginal nations and rather focuses on Western art.

15

A) 2spc/NM/NI: "surprising" does not work since the passage states that aboriginal cultures have their own interpretations of lore surrounding "The Dreaming." We are looking for a word that is similar to "expected," or perhaps "unique."

B) 2spc: "unremarkable" has a negative connotation and is a judgment of quality or character. This type of judgment does not fit the context of the passage, given that the author seems to be urging the appreciation of aboriginal cultures.

C) 2spc/NI: "problematic" is incorrect for reasons similar to answer choice b. The negative connotation is unjustified.

D) **ANSWER: "Characteristic" fits well, since we would expect aboriginal cultures to have their own interpretations of "The Dreaming" given the content of the passage.**

16

A) NI: The "intentions" of the non-Indigenous are not the subject of discussion; rather the discussion is about how to judge appropriately.

B) Opp: If anything, the author suggests that judgments made by non-Indigenous people may be problematic.

C) **ANSWER: This is the correct answer, since the author claims that the viewer requires a different framework for approaching aboriginal art, thus the viewpoint of non-Indigenous people is "limited."**

D) 2spc: "impossible" is too extreme, and furthermore judgments cannot be "impossible."

17

A) NI/NM: These lines do not discuss the judgment of non-indigenous people.

B) NI/NM: These lines introduce cultural differences, but do not discuss the non-indigenous people.

C) NI/NM: Similar to the problem with answer choice A, this does not discuss the non-indigenous judgments.

D) **ANSWER: This is correct because it demonstrates that the judgment of non-Indigenous people may be limited.**

18

A) **ANSWER: This is the best answer choice, since "collective" is should be contrasted with the "self" in the sentence.**

B) contender, 2spc: Although composite is definitely appealing since it means "made up of various different parts," composite generally refers to inanimate objects. Since the sentence is discussing people, communal is the better fit.

C) NI: "augmented" means enhanced, and we need a word that contrasts with "self" or individual.

D) NI: "concentrated" has similar problems similar to answer choice C.

19

A) NI/NM: "misconception" is the danger word, and the author does not discuss any misconceptions in these lines.

B) NI/NM: no competing claim is being made, so there is nothing to "disprove."

C) NI/NM: no "widely-held belief" is discussed, therefore it cannot be "challenged" either.

D) **ANSWER: The conception of self contrasts with the collective sense of identity as discussed in the sentences.**

20

A) NI: the relationship of a key and lock suggest an answer and a secret, which is unrelated to the discussion of self and communal in the last paragraph.

B) **ANSWER: This choice works best because a "puzzle" is a single component, whereas the nation as a whole is the "completed puzzle."**

C) NI: Needle and thread can be interpreted as two objects that work together, and is unrelated to the discussion of self and communal in the last paragraph.

D) NI: A book and its table of contents suggests the relationship between content and headers for content, which is not the focus of this paragraph.

21

A) **ANSWER: This answer choice is correct based on the chart, since all other cultures have categories with 0%, whereas the prehistoric Australians use all the symbols.**

B) NM: We know nothing about "religious ceremonies" based on the chart.

C) opp: some cultures use 0%.

D) NM-NI: Based on the chart, we do not know which symbols can be "permanently etched into the environment."

Passage 3

22

A) NI: Although this answer choice is partially discussed in the passage, it does not discuss the relationship between beech scale and fungi mentioned in this sentence.

B) NI: Although this is most likely true, the relationship between scale and fungi is not discussed.

C) NI: Similar to the problem with answer choice b. Although this is most likely true, the relationship between scale and fungi is not discussed.

D) **ANSWER: This choice accurately captures the interaction between scale and fungi through the word "predisposes."**

23

A) **ANSWER: Since "bitterly cold conditions" is the opposite of temperate climates, this answer choice would fully contradict and disprove the student's claim.**

B) opp: this answer choice supports the student's claim instead of contradicting it.

C) NM/NI: The range of attack has nothing to do with the focus on climate.

D) opp: Similar to B, this answer choice partially supports the student's claim about temperate climates and fungi.

24

A) 2spc/opp: "confirmed" is too extreme of a word, and the passage claims that milder winters would help propagate scale and fungi.

B) **ANSWER: The author discusses how geographical variables might help beech populations, but is quick to offset these with the potential costs that climate change brings. Thus, this is the best answer.**

C) NI/NM: there must be at least two hypotheses for there to be an "alternate hypothesis," but this is not the case.

D) NI/opp: Although this answer choice is partially discussed, the author claims that the benefits of beech migration may be offset by climate change.

25

A) NI/2gen: Although "droughts" are mentioned in this paragraph, droughts are mentioned only in relation to the nitrogen content, so this answer choice falls short.

B) opp: old growth trees are preferred, thus they are not "advantageous."

C) ANSWER: Since the author is discussing the link between lower nitrogen levels and bark preference, this is our best answer choice.

D) 2gen: This answer choice fails to discuss nitrogen levels, and instead sweeps them under a single banner of "chemical compositions" which is too broad. Compositions is also plural, whereas we are interested in only nitrogen.

26

A) NI/2spc: The qualitative comparison between European and American management techniques is not the issue.

B) opp: This answer choice confuses the causality of temperature and beech populations. Lower temperatures might help stabilize beech populations, not the other way around.

C) NM: "water" is not mentioned in the discussion of thinning down certain trees.

D) ANSWER: "thinning" best matches with "selective removal" in the answer choice.

27

A) NM: Resistance efforts in America are not mentioned; here the author is providing hypothetical solutions.

B) opp: The author is implying that beech populations can survive if appropriate measures are implemented.

C) ANSWER: The words are imply potential threats and the magnitude of BBD, thus this is our best answer choice.

D) NI: Which pathogens BBD favors is besides the point of these words or the paragraph.

28

A) NM: severely diseased never gets to the level of 66%

B) ANSWER: Correct based on the graph

C) severely diseased trees are below 50%, so 55% is inaccurate.

D) 10% is too low of an estimate.

29

A) NM: The most recent points shows that 75% are dead, so the range 75-95% is incorrect.

B) ANSWER: This choice is an accurate interpretation of the graph and supports the statement in the question.

C) NI: Although this choice is factually correct, it fails to provide information on recent data.

D) 2gen/NM: This is graphically incorrect for a number of years and the answer choice does not mention a specific year.

30

A) NI: in some years, both figures combined are less than 50%

B) NM: Although this answer choice is close, the question 29 asks for "currently" and this is not the most current data.

C) Similar problem to answer choice B.

D) ANSWER: Correct based on the graph

31

A) NI: Although tempting, the graph does not show us the severity of infection, so we cannot choose A.

B) NI: This answer choice has no relevance to death of beech trees.

C) NI: These lines are focused on geography in relation to infestation, not number of deaths.

D) **ANSWER: Since the graph shows that beech trees are on a dying trend, this answer choice is supported.**

Passage 4

32

A) 2spc: "value" is the danger word in this answer choice. Although value is implied in the passage, the passage primarily focuses on why America should engage in space exploration, not the "value" to be gained behind such exploration.

B) **ANSWER: "Undertaking" is synonymous for space exploration, so this is our best answer choice. "Urgency" is a strong word, but is justified based on the passage since Kennedy claims that America is behind in the race, and that the undertaking is important.**

C) 2spc/NI: "feasibility" is the danger word here. The passage does not focus on whether space exploration is logistically possible, but claims that America will participate and lead the process.

D) 2spc: "question" is the danger word here. Although the passage does certainly discuss "underlying motives" for space exploration (the fact that space is the new, unknown frontier and thus exploration is important), the passage never "questions" this assumption. Rather, the passage takes exploration as a given and attempts to persuade the audience to support space exploration.

33

A) 2spc: "scientists" is the danger word here. Although scientists are mentioned in the 1st paragraph, the overall focus is not on scientists, but rather the entire nation's effort towards space exploration. Furthermore, "immense" is a danger word that is not justified based on the passage. There are certainly going to be implied difficulties, but "immense" is too strong.

B) 2spc/NI: "most difficult," "all" are both too extreme for the passage. Furthermore, although the passage says that America intends to lead the space exploration process, that motivation does not lie in the will to "assert dominance," a phrase which adds an unwarranted negative connotation.

C) **ANSWER: This choice appropriately encompasses the "American people" and the objective of "becoming the leading nation of the space age." This answer choice is appropriately broader in scope compared to answer choice A) This is the best choice.**

D) 2spc/NM: "full responsibility" is too extreme in this context. Furthermore, there is no mention of warfare in the passage.

34

A) 2spc, contender: Although this answer choice is tempting, the repetition of the phrase "we" is not best understood as a call for "immediate" action. Immediate is too specific in this context.

B) **ANSWER: Since "we" refers to Americans and**

the speech is addressed to Americans, it is fair to interpret this repetition as an appeal to patriotism. Therefore, "solidarity" is a good fit.

C) 2spc: "familial bond" goes a bit too far. Although the passage emphasizes commonalities shared and embraced by Americans, the passage does not emphasize a family unit.

D) NI: "bravery" is not a focal point in this passage and does not fit the context properly.

35

A) **ANSWER: The discussion in the first paragraph lends itself towards humanity's technological progression, so this is our best choice.**

B) 2spc/NI: "criticize" is the danger word, and does not fit the context of this passage. The primary intention of the passage is to persuade Americans that space exploration is necessary, not to criticize.

C) 2spc/NM: "scarred by war" is the danger word, and this is not mentioned at all. A student who chooses this answer choice most likely applied outside knowledge of U.S. history inappropriately.

D) NI: To "honor the legacy" is not the main point of this passage, nor is "technological development." The author is arguing that space exploration is necessary, therefore this answer choice falls short.

36

A) NI/2spc: "required" is the danger word, and is too extreme. Furthermore, "earn their respect" is besides the point of the passage.

B) **ANSWER: This is our best answer choice since Kennedy discusses how the previous generation of Americans have paved the way for a bright future.**

C) NI/NM: "preventing cooperation among America's enemies" adds an unwarranted sinister and negative connotation that the passage does not discuss.

D) 2spc/NM: "dependent" is a powerful word, and should be carefully considered. Furthermore, the relationships between "new jobs" and the space age is not clearly established in the passage.

37

A) NI: These lines talk about space exploration, but do not discuss "leading other nations." Thus it does not answer what question 36 is asking.

B) **ANSWER: "Those who came before us" is synonymous in this context is "American forefathers." These lines also discuss leadership. This is the best answer choice.**

C) contender, NI: Although these lines are tempting because they discuss leadership. However, since they do not discuss "America's forefathers," this cannot be the correct answer choice.

D) NI: These lines do not discuss American leadership.

38

A) contender, 2spc: "guaranteed" is too specific for this passage. If exploration were "guaranteed" there would be no reason for the passage to argue that we need to explore space.

B) NI/NM: "disturbing" does not fit the discussion of the passage. The passage describes space exploration as a difficult but manageable endeavor.

C) **ANSWER: Since space exploration is understood to be difficult, "daunting" is a good synonym. "Uncompromising" is also a good synonym since the author is claiming that Americans must participate and lead space exploration.**

D) NI: "strange" is an inappropriate word for this passage. Space exploration is deemed difficult but beneficial, not "strange."

39

A) NI: These lines do not discuss difficulty or dedication to space exploration. It discusses how America can remain in a position of leadership.

B) NI: These lines do not discuss the difficulty or dedication to space exploration, rather it discusses how American influence can determines whether this new frontier will be peaceful or war-ridden.

C) **ANSWER: This is our best choice since "hard" is a good synonym for "daunting," and "we are unwilling to postpone" fits well with "uncompromising."**

D) contender, 2spc: Although this choice discusses "uncompromising," by stating that "we do not intend to stay behind," it lacks the focus of "daunting." Therefore, the answer choice falls a bit short.

40

A) Opp/NI: The sentence is hinting at the fact that much like previous American innovations and leadership, America does not intend to stay behind. "Opportunity" is thus the opposite of backwash.

B) **ANSWER: The sentence discusses how America does not intend to be left behind. Therefore, "backwash" is a good fit with "aftermath."**

C) Opp/NI: This answer choice has similar problems to answer choice A.

D) 2spc: "Flood" is perhaps too literal of an understanding of backwash.

41

A) 2spc: "scientists" is too specific to describe the purpose of these lines, since the passage as a whole is arguing that space exploration requires the effort of all Americans.

B) 2spc/NI: These lines do not hint at the "demand" for new knowledge or technology. They show to illustrate that exploration of new frontiers can be difficult, as shown through Malloy's death.

C) **ANSWER: This is the best choice. "Ambitious" is a good fit, since much like Malloy's death, space exploration will demand similar dedication.**

D) 2spc/opp: "enjoyable" is a danger word in this answer choice. If anything, exploration is portrayed as difficult and potentially dangerous, as shown by Malloy's death. Thus, "enjoyable" does not fit the context. Furthermore, "American explorers" is too specific to encapsulate space exploration as a whole.

Passage 5

42

A) NI/2spc: "evidence" is the danger word, and mentioning amino acids does not function as evidence. Amino acids are mentioned as a derivative benefit of skeletal muscle mass.

B) NM: "weight" is not mentioned in relation to amino acids.

C) NI: Although the author does discuss the advantages of increased protein ingestion, this is not related to the discussion of amino acids.

D) ANSWER: This choice captures the link between skeletal mass and amino acids.

43

A) NM: The relationship between protein intake and metabolism is not discussed in the passage.

B) ANSWER: Since the passage indicates that too much protein can cause stress to the body, this is a good fit with "undue strain."

C) 2spc: Although the relationship between protein intake and anabolic resistance is discussed, "promote further" is too specific.

D) NM: This answer choice specifically targets "the elderly," which is not discussed in the passage.

44

A) NI/2gen: These lines discuss the importance of protein and skeletal muscle mass in general terms, without referring to the link between protein and bodily stress.

B) NI: These lines discuss skeletal muscle mass, not protein intake.

C) NI: These lines discuss the limits of protein intake, not the link between protein consumption and stress on the body.

D) ANSWER: "unwanted load" is a good synonym for "undue strain." Furthermore, these lines discussion protein intake. This is the best choice.

45

A) 2spc: Since "sedentary" is used in contrast with active bodybuilders and trainers, "subdued" does not work for this context.

B) 2spc: Although "inert" does refer to a lack of action, it is too extreme since "inert" means something along the lines of "unable to move."

C) ANSWER: This is the best choice. It captures the contrast set up in the sentence between active and inactive.

D) NI: "apathetic" is directed towards emotional situations, whereas the sentence is discussing physical activity.

46

A) NM: no "question" is mentioned in the previous paragraph, therefore the discussion of muscle full cannot provide an alternative solution.

B) 2spc: the concept of muscle full is not an "example," but rather a phenomenon that is related to the discussion in the previous paragraph.

C) ANSWER: This is the best choice since it demonstrates that the relationship between protein intake and skeletal muscle mass is not straightforward, thus "limits" is a good fit.

D) NI/NM: There is no "metaphor" in the previous paragraph. The paragraphs are discussing real biological phenomenon, not metaphorical ones.

47

A) **ANSWER: The relationship between pre-sleep protein intake and overnight muscle synthesis is the central discussion of this passage. Therefore, this is the best choice.**

B) 2spc: "it alone" is too extreme in this context. Since other potential post-exercise synthesis methods are not discussed, "it alone" cannot be justified.

C) NM: The discussion of "amino acids" is more pertinent to the first passage.

D) 2spc/NM: The passage does not discuss the "commercial viability" of pre-sleep protein ingestion.

48

A) 2spc: We are looking for a word that describes a single "workout routine." There is no element of contest or competition hinted at in the sentence.

B) 2spc: "encounter" does not fit the context since the sentence is describing exercise, not meeting someone of something.

C) This answer choice has similar problems to answer choice a. There is no element of competition involved, so "match" is inappropriate.

D) **ANSWER: This is the best choice, since we are looking for a word that can describe something like "one exercise routine." Session fits well.**

49

A) NI/2spc: Passage 2 and Passage 1 are talking about related phenomenon, but are not disagreeing with one another. Therefore, it is incorrect to claim that P2 "disproves" P1.

B) **ANSWER: Since Passage 2 is certainly more detailed (it focuses exclusively on workouts), this is our best answer choice.**

C) 2spc: This answer choice has similar problems with answer choice a. Since the two passages are not written in direct relation to one another, P2 is not "arguing against" P1.

D) NM: There is no "doubt" mentioned in P2. There is also no "proposal" in P1.

50

A) NM: Since passage 2 does not discuss "slow" or "fast" proteins, this cannot be our answer.

B) 2spc: "most" is too specific. Although overnight sleep is certainly important to passage 2, we cannot substantiate "most."

C) NM: The "frequency of ingestion" is not discussed in passage 2.

D) **ANSWER: Since this is a central claim that passage 2 is making, this is the best answer choice.**

51

A) NI: These lines do not discuss post-exercise muscle protein synthesis, and thus cannot be our answer.

B) NI: These lines do not discuss the "slow" and "fast" different proteins, although they do discuss post-exercise muscle protein synthesis. This answer choice falls a bit short.

C) **ANSWER: This is the best answer choice since it discusses both post-exercise muscle protein synthesis and "type" of protein ingestion, referring to slow and fast proteins.**

D) NI: These lines do not discuss both the protein or post-exercise synthesis.

52

A) 2spc: The quantity of amino acids is not implied in P1 or P2.

B) **ANSWER: Lines 80 shows the explicit claim in P2. The claim is implicit in P1 based on line 12, since amino acids can help the body recover in general.**

C) NM: The relationship between amino acids and overnight synthesis rates is not discussed in P1.

D) NM: This answer choice has similar problems with answer choice a. The quantity of amino acids is not discussed.

Part 1

SAT® Practice Test #2

Reading Test

65 MINUTES, 52 QUESTIONS

Turn to Section 1 of your answer sheet to answer the questions in this section.

DIRECTIONS

Each passage or pair of passages below is followed by a number of questions. After reading each passage or pair, choose the best answer to each question based on what is stated or implied in the passage or passages and in any accompanying graphics (such as a table or graph).

Questions 1-10 are based on the following passage.

This passage is excerpt from *The Count of Monte Cristo* by Alexandre Dumas. Originally published in 1844.

As Danglars approached Fernand, he cast on the disappointed lover a look of deep meaning, while Fernand himself slowly paced behind Mercédès and
Line Dantès, the happy pair who seemed, in their own
5 unmixed content, to have entirely forgotten that such a being as himself existed. Fernand was pale and abstracted; occasionally, however, a deep flush would overspread his countenance, and a nervous contraction distort his features, while, with an agitated and
10 restless gaze, he would glance in the direction of the night-shrouded city behind them, like one who either anticipated or foresaw some great and important event.

Dantès was simply, but becomingly, clad in the dress peculiar to the merchant service—a costume
15 somewhat between a military and a civil garb; and with his fine countenance, radiant with joy and happiness, a more perfect specimen of manly beauty could scarcely be imagined.

Lovely as the Greek girls of Cyprus or Chios,
20 Mercédès boasted the same bright flashing eyes of jet, and ripe, round, coral lips. One more practiced in the arts of great cities would have hid her blushes beneath a veil, or, at least, have cast down her thickly fringed lashes, so as to have concealed the
25 liquid lustre of her animated eyes; but, on the contrary, the delighted girl looked around her with a smile that seemed to say: "If you are my friends, rejoice with me, for I am very happy."

As soon as this bridal party came in sight of La
30 Réserve, M. Morrel descended and came forth to meet it, followed by the soldiers and sailors there assembled. Dantès, at the approach of his patron, respectfully placed the arm of his affianced bride within that of M. Morrel, who, forthwith conducting
35 her up the flight of wooden steps leading to the chamber in which the feast was prepared, was gayly followed by the guests, beneath whose heavy tread the slight structure creaked and groaned for the space of several minutes.

40 "Father," said Mercédès, stopping when she had reached the centre of the table, "sit, I pray you, on my right hand; on my left I will place him who has ever been as a brother to me," pointing with a soft and gentle smile to Fernand; but her words and look
45 seemed to inflict the direst torture on him, for his lips became ghastly pale, and even beneath the dark hue of his complexion the blood might be seen retreating as though some sudden pang drove it back to the heart.

50 "A pretty silence truly!" said the old father of the bridegroom, as he carried to his lips a glass of wine of the hue and brightness of the topaz, and which had just been placed before Mercédès herself. "Now, would anybody think that this room contained a
55 happy, merry party, who desire nothing better than to laugh and dance the hours away?"

"Ah," sighed Dantès' friend Caderousse, "a man cannot always feel happy because he is about to be married."

"The truth is," replied Dantès, "that I am too happy for noisy mirth; if that is what you meant by your observation, my worthy friend, you are right; joy takes a strange effect at times, it seems to oppress us almost the same as sorrow."

Danglars looked towards Fernand, whose excitable nature received and betrayed each fresh impression.

"Why, what ails you?" asked Danglars of Dantès. "Do you fear any approaching evil? I should say that you were the happiest man alive at this instant."

"And that is the very thing that alarms me," returned Dantès. "Man does not appear to me to be intended to enjoy felicity so unmixed; happiness is like the enchanted palaces we read of in our childhood, where fierce, fiery dragons defend the entrance and approach; and monsters of all shapes and kinds, requiring to be overcome ere victory is ours. I own that I am lost in wonder to find myself promoted to an honor of which I feel myself unworthy—that of being the husband of Mercédès."

"Nay, nay!" cried Caderousse, smiling, "you have not attained that honor yet. Mercédès is not yet your wife. Just assume the tone and manner of a husband, and see how she will remind you that your hour is not yet come!"

The bride blushed, while Fernand, restless and uneasy, seemed to start at every fresh sound, and from time to time wiped away the large drops of perspiration that gathered on his brow.

1

The primary purpose of the opening paragraph of the passage is to
A) contrast a character's words with his inner thoughts.
B) establish the narrator's position in a conflict.
C) offer a symbolic representation of one man's struggle.
D) provide context for understanding one character's emotional state.

2

During the course of the first three paragraphs, the focus shifts from
A) one man's memories to his understanding of a present situation.
B) a young couple's excitement about the future to a third person's reflections on marriage.
C) one character's internal conflict to the discussion of a happy couple.
D) the assessment of one man's motivations to those of a young couple.

3

Which choice best summarizes the second half of the passage?
A) Two characters fight over the love of one woman.
B) A character pauses during a celebration to consider how he feels.
C) A disappointed suitor realizes he will not achieve the love he seeks.
D) A young man has reservations on the eve of his marriage.

4

The reference to the "arts of great cities" in line 22 primarily has which effect?
A) It underscores Mercédès' charm and innocence.
B) It reveals Mercédès' longing for a return to city life.
C) It evokes Mercédès' shyness and timidity.
D) It captures Mercédès' distaste for pretense.

5

The passage implies that Fernand's behavior is mainly caused by his
A) contempt for Dantès' humble background.
B) impatience with Mercédès' excessive celebration.
C) indignation at Mercédès' impulsive actions.
D) dismay over Mercédès' romantic decision.

6

The passage indicates that Mercédès views Fernand as a
A) former lover.
B) shrewd rival.
C) close companion.
D) fellow conspirator.

7

Which choice provides the best evidence for the answer to the previous question?
A) Lines 1-7 ("As Danglars...abstracted")
B) Lines 40-44 ("Father...Fernand")
C) Lines 44-49 ("but...heart")
D) Lines 85-88 ("The bride...brow")

8

Dantès' comparison of joy to sorrow mainly has the effect of

A) highlighting a seeming paradox.
B) reconciling opposing concepts.
C) conveying the intensity of his reservations.
D) foreshadowing the eventual end of a relationship.

9

The passage indicates that Dantès sometimes finds happiness to be

A) unbearable.
B) chaotic.
C) constant.
D) burdensome.

10

Which choice provides the best evidence for the answer to the previous question?

A) Lines 57-59 ("Ah...married")
B) Lines 63-64 ("joy...sorrow")
C) Lines 71-72 ("Man...unmixed")
D) Lines 80-81 ("Nay...yet")

Questions 11-21 are based on the following passage and supplementary material.

This passage is adapted from *Noise in Schools: A Holistic Approach to the Issue*, Pamela Woolner and Elaine Hall, 2010.

   Much of the extensive research relating to the issue of noise in education has focused on relating noise levels to particular outcomes. Notably, the results, using both experimental and observational methodologies, are remarkably consistent. The findings show that noisy conditions have direct negative effects on learning, as well as causing indirect problems to learners through distractions or annoyances. The finding that chronic noise exposure impairs cognitive functioning is of particular concern to education professionals. Studies have found associations between noisy environments and reading problems, deficiencies in pre-reading skills and other general cognitive deficits. There is the implication that in addition to interfering with processing in any given occasion, environmental noise may contribute to developmental problems, particularly with speech, language, and reading. These studies imply that either living in a home or attending a school near a source of ongoing noise will increase the likelihood of a child having educational difficulties.

   However, recent research into the problem of noise in school environments has tended to center on the more widespread problem of students struggling to learn because of noise generated within the school itself. Possibly problematic noise comes from several sources, as demonstrated in studies where measurements of classroom noise levels were made. Firstly, there is noise intrusion, which can come from outside the school, but seems to be increased more by noise from other parts of the school leaking into the classroom. Secondly, there is background noise from within the room, often due to heating and ventilation systems but also caused by equipment such as projectors and computers. Finally there is the noise generated by students engaged in learning, which, unsurprisingly, varies according to the nature of the activity. Noise levels are argued to be exacerbated by high levels of reverberation (echoing), since this can increase the noise level itself and make the hearing of speech more difficult. The consistent findings, across laboratory and field studies, of noise interfering with language based tasks together with concerns about speech intelligibility in the classroom has suggested to some that controlling reverberation might be as important as reducing noise levels.

   One study involved a series of experiments where school children read texts in either noisy or quiet conditions, with the noise provided by recordings of aircraft, train and road noise, or irrelevant speech. Tests conducted a week later in quiet conditions showed deficits in memory for these texts when they were studied in noisy conditions, with this being more pronounced for recall, as opposed to recognition, of information. Interestingly, this deficiency in learning continued from session to session when children had experienced noise first, associated with motivation for the task dropping off as a result of the noise experience. Thus, these sorts of experiments demonstrate not only that children generally have more difficulty performing cognitive tasks when it is noisy, but also that noise tends to undermine long term learning, corroborating the findings of the observational studies of chronic environmental noise.

   It is clear that a range of approaches to noise problems in school are required. Appropriate solutions will depend partly on the nature of the noise, with differing solutions needed for different sorts of noise. The impact of external noise on health and happiness, as well on learning, has distinct implications for the planning and architecture of schools. Noise leaking between rooms suggests improved sound insulation while high levels of background noise in classrooms indicate a need for quieter models of heating, cooling, and ventilation. Yet it is also clear that solutions to noise in school will differ according to which causal factors are emphasized. It can be seen that a narrow view of the physical aspects of a learning environment may be sufficient to unveil the negative effects of noise on learning. Yet a wider perspective will be necessary to avoid producing detrimental effects on health and wellbeing, as well as on some of the wide range of actions that comprise learning.

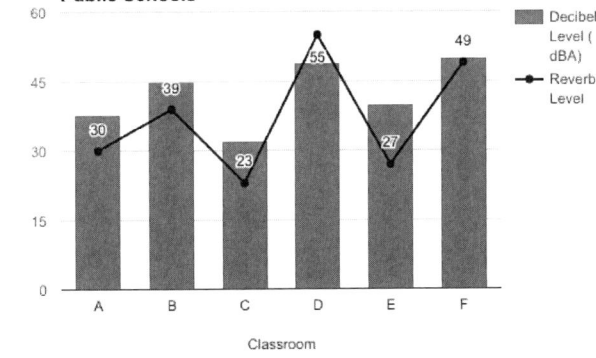

Chart adapted from *Noise in Schools: A Holistic Approach to the Issue* by Pamela Woolner and Elaine Hall, 2010.

11

The main purpose of the passage is to
A) consider the link between poverty and academic performance.
B) argue that identifying solutions to eliminate noise will improve health.
C) describe the primary factors that lead to poor cognitive function.
D) examine the impact of noise exposure on learning environments.

12

The author suggests which of the following situations will lead to increased educational problems?
A) Annoying noises will irritate students in a learning environment and increase the likelihood of conflict.
B) Living in a chronically noisy environment will likely increase the negative effects on learning.
C) Heating and ventilation systems will continue to be the largest sources of distraction in the classroom.
D) Children's long term learning will suffer as long as they fail to recall and recognize information.

13

Which choice provides the best evidence for the answer to the previous question?
A) Lines 5-8 ("The findings...annoyances")
B) Lines 18-21 ("These...difficulties")
C) Lines 26-28 ("Possibly...made")
D) Lines 51-55 ("Tests...information")

14

As used in line 23, "center" most nearly means
A) pivot.
B) focus.
C) average.
D) converge.

15

The main purpose of the third paragraph (lines 47-64) is to
A) provide support for the argument that high noise levels lead to permanent damage.
B) illustrate that children struggle more with recognition than with recall.
C) reveal that noise intrusions have harmful effects on cognitive processing.
D) give examples of the economic problems caused by real world noises.

16

As used in line 54, "pronounced" most nearly means
A) enunciated.
B) precise.
C) articulated.
D) noticeable.

17

Which choice best supports the author's claim that student-generated noise is harmful?
A) Lines 14-18 ("There...reading")
B) Lines 29-32 ("Firstly...classroom")
C) Lines 32-35 ("Secondly...computers")
D) Lines 35-41 ("Finally...difficult")

18

The primary purpose of the final paragraph (lines 65-83) is to argue that
A) architectural practices need to be updated and standardized in order to remove noise intrusions.
B) understanding noise in schools may improve students' health and education.
C) deciding upon the best solutions for noise problems in different locations will remain a challenge for learning environments.
D) school buildings should be constructed from the start with high quality sound insulation to combat external noises.

19

Data in the graph about background noise levels and corresponding reverberation levels most strongly support which of the following statements?
A) The reverberation level amongst all six classrooms did not vary greatly.
B) Classroom E displayed the lowest reverberation level despite a noise level above 30 dBA.
C) The highest reverberation levels corresponded with noise levels at or above 45 dBA.
D) The low reverberation level of Classroom C led to the sudden increase in the reverberation level of Classroom D.

20

Data in the graph indicate that the smallest difference between noise levels and reverberation levels occurred in which classroom?
A) Classroom B
B) Classroom C
C) Classroom D
D) Classroom F

21

Data in the graph provide most direct support for which idea in the passage?
A) Noisy environments can lead to hearing damage.
B) Noise levels can increase due to high reverberation levels.
C) Reverberation can decrease cognitive functioning.
D) Noise leaking can lead to increased reverberation within classrooms.

Questions 22-32 are based on the following passages.

Passage 1 is adapted from *What's in a Name?* by Sune Borkfelt, 2011. Passage 2 is adapted from *I Felt Like My Life Had Been Given to Me to Start Over* by Eleonora Rao, 2016.

Passage 1

Naming is the very first and most basic act of language, because it enables us to talk or write about something in specific terms, whether the object named is human or non-human, animate or inanimate. However, naming is not as uncomplicated as we may usually think and names have consequences for the way we think about animals, people, species, places, and things. When naming an individual animal or a species, we not only choose how we want to represent that animal, but also how others are to represent and perceive it, as we see the world. This makes naming a powerful tool of control.

With categorizations of non-human animals, however, we might argue the practice has been taken to its extreme. Indeed, using the very term 'animal' to bundle together all other species is perhaps the most extreme example of generic naming in terms of how many differences there are between the creatures defined by it. And the exclusion of ourselves from that same generic term, by viewing the word 'human' as an opposite to it, is as arbitrary as would be the exclusion of any other species. Moreover, as Tim Ingold argues, all the qualities we as humans are claimed to "uniquely have, the animal is consequently supposed to lack; thus, the generic concept of 'animal' is negatively constituted by the sum of those deficiencies." As a consequence, being an 'animal' becomes intrinsically negative.

Other categorizations work in similar ways. We regard, and treat, animals differently, depending on the category they belong to. Thus, for instance, what is thought of as the proper way of treating a rabbit may differ remarkably depending on whether we have labelled it as a 'pet', as 'vermin', as a 'food animal' or as a 'research subject.' Thus, labelling and categorizing can give us the power of applying non-humans to different and often contrasting uses without taking the arbitrariness of such a practice into account.

When we name, we are thus in fact exercising a power over the animals we name. For while naming can be said to be a necessity for language and communication, the very act of naming actually makes animals into objects, which we choose how to perceive, represent and categorize through the names we apply to them. On the other hand, not naming can mean distancing ourselves from other animals and disregarding their likeness to ourselves, which makes it easier to justify harmful treatment through reference to the difference between 'them' and 'us.' Which may especially be the case if we choose to apply a label or categorization instead of a name and classify animals as, for instance, 'vermin' or 'research animal.' Indeed, not just denying individual names, but also ignoring the names of species, can help hide a practice, which is harmful to animals: words such as 'bacon' and 'ham', for instance, may help us ignore the fact that it is in fact an animal, a 'pig,' we are eating.

Passage 2

Alice Kaplan's *French Lessons: A Memoir* is a story that deals as much with the issue of language learning as with that of cultural belonging(s). This "language memoir" is an intimate tale of the transition between languages and cultures. In French Lessons the narrator attempts to relate accounts of her experience rather than expertise in language learning. She reflects on multiple aspects of learning a second language, such as the differences in emotional tenor between the new and old languages, or the way language functions differently for each personality type within a given collection of words and grammar. "Each person approaches the intersection of language mechanics and emotion in a different way. The words we choose (or are able to choose) to express ourselves differ greatly amongst languages," Kaplan writes.

French Lessons also explores Kaplan's passion for another language and another way of life. To return to her essay "On Language Memoirs" where Kaplan looks into the psychological repercussions of living immersed in another language, she observes: "There is no language change without emotional consequences. Principally: loss. That language equals home, that language is a home, and that to be without a language, or to be between languages, is as miserable as to be without bread." She recounts her experience of sensing the birth of a new persona: "I hid in my second language, where I leaped out of myself."

To speak a foreign language is to depart from one's self. "Language memoirs are closest in genre to the
90 classic *Bildungsroman*—the novel of education and development. The difference is that it's not yourself you're growing into, but another self, perceived as better, more powerful, safer. The change in language is the emblem of a leap into a new persona." In this
95 laborious process of discovery and transformation writing plays a crucial part. Kaplan underscores that she has to find the right form for her memoir. Through the acts of memoir, memory can be rendered into what Kaplan calls "scenes of language" and into
100 writing. This act of writing, Kaplan highlights in *French Lessons*, "isn't a straight line but a process where you have to get in trouble to get anywhere. Because I was disturbed, it was better writing than any I had done before." She needs to regain contact
105 with her emotions and the writing of the memoir provides a privileged access. Ultimately, the homecoming is the writing of the memoir itself.

22

The author of Passage 1 indicates which of the following about the act of naming?
A) It brings us closer to inanimate objects.
B) It carries certain repercussions.
C) It promotes racist sentiments.
D) It should be further simplified.

23

Which choice provides the best evidence for the answer to the previous question?
A) Lines 1-4 ("Naming...inanimate")
B) Lines 5-8 ("However...things")
C) Lines 15-19 ("Indeed...it")
D) Lines 27-28 ("As...negative")

24

The author of Passage 1 indicates that not naming can
A) improve people's self-awareness.
B) increase human contact with animals.
C) undermine other animals' abilities to feel.
D) estrange people from non-human animals.

25

As used in line 32, "proper" most nearly means
A) formal.
B) strict.
C) suitable.
D) decorous.

26

In Passage 2, Alice Kaplan refers to the *Bildungsroman* mainly to suggest that she
A) dislikes the Bildungsroman as a genre.
B) has become quite skilled at writing in a second language.
C) has had to mature through language.
D) regrets having learned such a difficult language.

27

According to the author of Passage 2, what do language memoirs and *Bildungsromans* have in common?
A) They encourage risk-taking in the development of identity.
B) They allow for personal growth and transformation.
C) They inspire curiosity in discerning readers.
D) They immerse the reader in their respective fields.

28

The metaphor in the final sentence of Passage 2 has mainly which effect?
A) It employs irony to poke fun at the human condition.
B) It encapsulates the views of the author and his subject.
C) It uses technical jargon to illustrate a complicated concept.
D) It alludes to the past to evoke a sense of belonging.

29

The primary purpose of each passage is to
A) consider the various implications of language.
B) make an argument about the benefits of bilingualism.
C) take a position on categorizing and labeling other species.
D) assess the creativity of individuals with varying levels of foreign language skills.

30

Which choice best describes the relationship between the two passages?
A) Passage 1 relates first-hand experiences that contrast with the analytical approach in Passage 2.
B) Passage 1 critiques the conclusions drawn from the memoir discussed in Passage 2.
C) Passage 1 explores the broader impact of a phenonomon while Passage 2 examines it from a personal context.
D) Passage 1 anticipates the reactions that the argument made in Passage 2 might elicit.

31

On which of the following points would the authors of both passages most likely agree?
A) Those who criticize the act of naming tend to overreact in their criticism.
B) Multilingual speakers tend to demonstrate more creativity overall.
C) Language in all its various contexts is a form of representation.
D) Understanding oneself is a necessary prerequisite to understanding others.

32

Which choice provides the best evidence that the author of Passage 2 would agree to some extent with the claim made in lines 8-11, Passage 1?
A) Lines 80-81 ("There...consequences")
B) Lines 82-85 ("That language...bread")
C) Lines 93-94 ("The change...persona")
D) Lines 98-100 ("Through...writing")

Questions 33-42 are based on the following passage and supplementary material.

This passage is excerpt from *"Military-Industrial Complex Speech"* by Dwight D. Eisenhower, 1961.

Throughout America's adventure in free government, our basic purposes have been to keep the peace; to foster progress in human achievement, and to enhance liberty, dignity and integrity among people and among
5 nations. To strive for less would be unworthy of a free people. Any failure traceable to arrogance, or our lack of comprehension or readiness to sacrifice would inflict upon us grievous hurt both at home and abroad.

Progress toward these noble goals is persistently
10 threatened by the conflict now engulfing the world. It commands our whole attention, absorbs our very beings. We face a hostile philosophy*—global in scope, ruthless in purpose, and insidious in method. To meet it successfully, there is called for, not so much
15 the emotional and temporary sacrifices of crisis, but rather those which enable us to carry forward steadily, surely, and without complaint the burdens of a prolonged and complex struggle—with liberty the stake. Only thus shall we remain, despite every provocation,
20 on our charted course toward permanent peace and human betterment.

Crises there will continue to be. In meeting them, whether foreign or domestic, great or small, there is a recurring temptation to feel that some spectacular and
25 costly action could become the miraculous solution to all current difficulties. A huge increase in newer elements of our defense; development of unrealistic programs to cure every ill in agriculture; a dramatic expansion in basic and applied research—these and
30 many other possibilities, each possibly promising in itself, may be suggested as the only way to the road we wish to travel.

But each proposal must be weighed in the light of a broader consideration: the need to maintain balance
35 in and among national programs — balance between the private and the public economy, balance between cost and hoped for advantage — balance between the clearly necessary and the comfortably desirable; balance between our essential requirements as a nation
40 and the duties imposed by the nation upon the individual; balance between actions of the moment and the national welfare of the future. Good judgment seeks balance and progress; lack of it eventually finds imbalance and frustration.

45 A vital element in keeping the peace is our military establishment. Our arms must be mighty, ready for instant action, so that no potential aggressor may be tempted to risk his own destruction. Until the latest of our world conflicts, the United States had no
50 armaments industry. But now we can no longer risk emergency improvisation of national defense; we have been compelled to create a permanent armaments industry of vast proportions. This conjunction of an immense military establishment and a large arms
55 industry is new in the American experience. The total influence—economic, political, even spiritual—is felt in every city, every State house, every office of Federal government. Yet we must not fail to comprehend its grave implications. Our toil, resources and livelihood
60 are all involved; so is the very structure of our society. In the councils of government, we must guard against the acquisition of unwarranted influence, whether sought or unsought, by the military industrial complex. The potential for the disastrous rise of
65 misplaced power exists and will persist. We must never let the weight of this combination endanger our liberties.

Akin to, and largely responsible for the sweeping changes in our industrial-military posture, has been the
70 technological revolution during recent decades. In this revolution, research has become central; it also becomes more formalized, complex, and costly. The prospect of domination of the nation's scholars by Federal employment, project allocations, and the power
75 of money is ever present and is gravely to be regarded. Yet, in holding scientific research and discovery in respect, we must also be alert to the equal and opposite danger that public policy could itself become the captive of a scientific technological
80 elite. It is the task of statesmanship to mold, to balance, and to integrate these and other forces, new and old, within the principles of our democratic system—ever aiming toward the supreme goals of our free society. As we peer into society's future, we—
85 you and I, and our government—must avoid the impulse to live only for today, plundering, for our own ease and convenience, the precious resources of tomorrow.

*Soviet Communism during the Cold War

33

The central danger that Eisenhower describes in the passage is that an industrial-military complex may
A) lead to an avoidable misuse of national resources.
B) fuel warfare between nations as a result of technological competition.
C) prevent the nation from upholding liberty, dignity, and integrity.
D) come to have an extensive influence over society.

34

Eisenhower uses the phrase "hostile philosophy" (line 12) mainly to emphasize what he sees as the
A) growing power of the national defense industry.
B) ideological threat of an international rival.
C) utter domination of society by the military.
D) regrettable decline in national morality.

35

Eisenhower claims that which of the following was a relatively recent historical development?
A) The technological changes of the Industrial Revolution
B) The manipulation of society by ideological forces
C) The creation of a permanent defense industry
D) The spread of war and injustice

36

Which choice provides the best evidence for the answer to the previous question?
A) Lines 1-5 ("Throughout...nations")
B) Lines 12-13 ("We...method")
C) Lines 48-50 ("Until...industry")
D) Lines 70-72 ("In...costly")

37

As used in line 11, "absorbs" most nearly means
A) consumes.
B) soaks.
C) includes.
D) digests.

38

Eisenhower contends that the situation he describes in the passage has become so widespread that there is an inclination to
A) become engrossed in the magnitude of global threats.
B) lament the conflicts that have been created.
C) seek idealistic solutions to do away with problems.
D) prompt opposing forces to compromise their own safety.

39

Which choice provides the best evidence for the answer to the previous question?
A) Lines 10-12 ("It...beings")
B) Lines 13-19 ("To...stake")
C) Lines 26-32 ("A huge...travel")
D) Lines 46-48 ("Our...destruction")

40

It can be reasonably inferred that "unwarranted influence" (line 63) was a term generally intended to
A) identify the consequence of a permanent armaments industry.
B) criticize the present misuse of power between the military and the government.
C) condemn the military industrial complex for increased governmental spending.
D) caution against unjustified control of the government by military interests.

41

As used in line 66, "weight" most nearly means
A) mass.
B) bulk.
C) burden.
D) quantity.

42

The sixth paragraph (lines 68-88) is most clearly establishes a contrast between
A) science and military.
B) power and money.
C) elitism and democracy.
D) the past and the future.

Questions 43-52 are based on the following passage and supplementary material.

This passage is excerpt from "Frog Swarms: Earthquake Precursors or False Alarms?" Rachel A. Grant and Hilary Conlan, 2013.

Unusual animal behavior prior to earthquakes has been reported for millennia but has rarely been scientifically documented. Recently, large migrations of amphibians have been linked to large earthquakes, and
5 media reports of large frog and toad migrations in areas of high seismic risk such as Greece and China have led to fears of a subsequent large earthquake. In China's Sichuan province, thousands of small toads were seen crossing a road, two days before the Great
10 Sichuan Earthquake in 2008. Other unusual behavior of amphibians has been linked to seismic activity; common toads abandoned spawning and left their breeding site five days before the L'Aquila, Italy earthquake in 2009 and only returned after the quake
15 had occurred.

Media reports linking unusual animal behavior with earthquakes can potentially create false alarms and unnecessary anxiety among people that live in earthquake risk zones. Largely because of these two
20 incidents, recent large amphibian migrations have triggered media speculation that they may be precursors to significant earthquakes. In particular, a mass migration of frogs in Thessaloniki, Greece, in 2010 gave rise to numerous media reports suggesting a
25 large earthquake was imminent in Greece or neighboring Turkey, but no earthquake occurred. Similarly, frog swarms occurring in Moratuwa, Sri Lanka, in 2010 also gave rise to earthquake fears, while in 2011 and 2012 several frog swarms caused
30 unfounded anxiety in Wuhan and Nanjing, China. Avoidance of false alarms is of utmost importance in short term earthquake risk forecasting to preclude panic among populations living in seismic risk areas.

Large migrations are part of the normal behavioral
35 repertoire of amphibians at certain times of the year. Many amphibians, particularly in temperate regions, breed in spring and their larvae metamorphose into juvenile frogs and toads in summer. In many cases, this metamorphosis and dispersal away from their birth
40 pond is synchronized, leading to large aggregations of tiny frogs or toads. Coordination of metamorphic and post-metamorphic groups are probably a defense against predation; large groups of animals moving together minimizes predation on the individual. Hence,
45 after a successful breeding season, it is not uncommon to see large numbers of tiny juvenile toads or frogs migrating from the breeding site and dispersing to terrestrial habitats. Where these coincide with roads or residential areas, they may find their way to media
50 reports as "frog swarms." In the temperate Northern hemisphere these aggregations normally occur in late spring or summer, shortly after metamorphosis has occurred. In dry climates a further migration may be seen in early autumn after estivation (the prolonged
55 dormancy of an animal after a hot period). Therefore, it is possible that frog swarms are not linked to large earthquakes, but are part of the normal migratory behavior of juvenile amphibians. If this is the case, they would be expected to occur primarily in summer,
60 and to consist of very small, uniformly sized amphibians. Frog swarms do not occur every year as they depend on numerous climatic and other factors and the size of many amphibian populations is highly variable from year to year.

65 News reports of "frog swarms" from 1850 to the present day were examined for evidence that this behavior is a precursor to large earthquakes. It was found that only two of 28 reported frog swarms preceded large earthquakes (Sichuan province, China
70 in 2008 and 2010). All of the reported mass migrations of amphibians occurred in late spring, summer, and autumn, and appeared to relate to small juvenile anurans (frogs and toads). It was concluded that most reported "frog swarms" are actually normal
75 behavior, probably caused by juvenile animals migrating away from their breeding pond, after a fruitful reproductive season. As amphibian populations undergo large fluctuations in numbers from year to year, this phenomenon will not occur on a yearly
80 basis but will depend on successful reproduction, which is related to numerous climatic and geophysical factors. In addition, it is likely that reports of several mass migrations of small toads prior to the Great Sichuan Earthquake in 2008 were not linked to the
85 subsequent 7.9 seismic event, and were probably coincidence. Further statistical analysis of the data indicate that frog swarms are unlikely to be connected with earthquakes. Reports of unusual behavior giving rise to earthquake fears should be interpreted with
90 caution, and consultation with experts in the field of earthquake biology is advised.

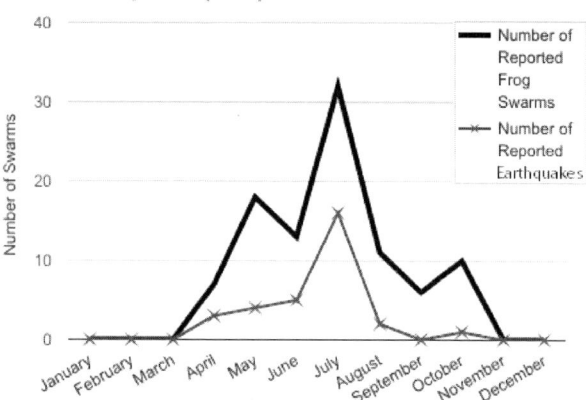

43

The first paragraph serves primarily to
A) describe how a scientific hypothesis was proven.
B) introduce a perceived connection.
C) outline media reports on an event.
D) explain the cause of two major earthquakes.

44

As used in line 17, "false" most nearly means
A) deceitful.
B) treacherous.
C) unfounded.
D) fictitious.

45

According to the passage, large amphibian migrations have triggered earthquake fears primarily because
A) frogs and toads can detect unusual seismic activity.
B) frogs and toads do not migrate in large groups unless there is imminent danger.
C) large amphibian migrations preceded two earthquakes in the past.
D) large amphibian migrations are often confused with "frog swarms."

46

Which choice provides the best evidence for the answer to the previous question?
A) Lines 3-7 ("Recently...earthquake")
B) Lines 19-22 ("Largely...earthquakes")
C) Lines 41-44 ("Coordination...individual")
D) Lines 48-50 ("Where...swarms")

47

As used in line 64, "variable" most nearly means
A) accidental.
B) changeable.
C) fleeting.
D) transitory.

48

Based on information in the passage, it can reasonably be inferred that irregular amphibian behavior
A) cannot be simply dismissed as it may be indicative of seismic activity.
B) can trigger emotional problems from excessive anxiety and stress.
C) is reflective of the immature tendencies of juvenile anuran amphibians.
D) may continue to be a source of popular media reports.

49

Which choice provides the best evidence for the answer to the previous question?
A) Lines 16-19 ("Media...zones")
B) Lines 22-26 ("In particular...occurred")
C) Lines 70-73 ("All...toads")
D) Lines 88-91 ("Reports...advised")

50

According to the graph, both the number of reported frog swarms and the number of reported earthquakes peaked at which month?

A) May
B) July
C) August
D) October

51

Which concept is supported by the passage and by the information in the graph?

A) Migratory behavior of frogs is dependent on successful reproductive seasons.
B) Frog swarms are not linked to earthquakes.
C) Massive migrations of amphibians typically occur during late spring and summer.
D) The timing of frog migrations is unpredictable.

52

How does the graph support the author's point that all reported mass migrations of amphibians took place during late spring, summer, and autumn?

A) It demonstrates that mass migrations are contingent on higher temperatures.
B) It illustrates that there is a high correlation between frog swarms and earthquakes during summer.
C) It reveals that large migrations are normative behaviors for juvenile frogs.
D) It shows that frog swarms occurred only between the months of April and October.

STOP

If you finish before time is called, you may check your work on this section only.
Do not turn to any other section.

Part 1

Practice Test 2: Answer Key and Explanations

Reading Test 2 Answer Key

Reading Test 2	
Question	Answer
1	D
2	C
3	B
4	A
5	D
6	C
7	B
8	A
9	D
10	B
11	D
12	B
13	B
14	B
15	C
16	D
17	D
18	B
19	C
20	D
21	B
22	B
23	B
24	D
25	C
26	C

Reading Test 2	
Question	Answer
27	B
28	B
29	A
30	C
31	C
32	A
33	D
34	B
35	C
36	C
37	A
38	C
39	C
40	D
41	C
42	C
43	B
44	C
45	C
46	B
47	B
48	A
49	D
50	B
51	C
52	D

*For self-scoring assessment tables, please turn to page 187.

Passage 1

1

A) NM: "character's words" - the character is not speaking in the paragraph

B) NM: "conflict" - no conflict is evident in the paragraph

C) NI: "symbolic" - no metaphor is apparent

D) ANSWER: All description is aimed at Fernand's emotions

2

A) NI: "memories" - paragraph 1 starts with the present

B) NI: "marriage" - paragraph 3 does not end with Fernand's thoughts on marriage

C) ANSWER: - from Danglar's thoughts to Dantes and Mercedes

D) NM: "motivations" - not made clear at any point

3

A) NM: "fight" - no fight is seen

B) ANSWER: Dantes is counting his blessings

C) NI: "disappointed suitor" Fernand is not the focus of the second half of the passage

D) NM: "reservations" - Dantes is not having reservations

4

A) NM/OPP: "innocence" is probably the opposite, "charm" - Y

B) NM: "longing for city life" - no implication is made

C) OPP: 'shyness and timidity' are the opposite

D) ANSWER: She does not "conceal" her emotions but is instead open and honest

5

A) NM: "humble" - not referenced, and "contempt" is 2STR

B) NM: "impatient" - the wrong emotion for the whole passage

C) NI: "impulsive" - Fernand is Y "indignant" but not impulsive

D) ANSWER: Line 2 "disappointed lover", but also a main idea of the passage

2

A) OPP: "lover" - she calls him "brother"

B) OPP: "rival" - they are close

C) ANSWER: "brother," in lines 40-44 implies that she considers him to be a close friend.

D) NM: "conspirator" - no secret plan is discussed

7

A) NI - the lines indicate Fernand's disappointment, the lovers' happiness and ignorance of his existence.

B) ANSWER: "as a brother to me" indicates that Mercedes considers Fernand to be very close, almost as kin.

C) NI - the lines show Fernand's reaction to Mercedes's statement. This does not answer the previous question.

D) NI - no mention of the relationship between Mercedes and Fernand.

8

A) NI: "paradox" - he does not say that some situation is self-denying

B) ANSWER: he is both happy and worried about

losing that happiness, thus less happy

C) OPP: "reservations" - he has none, he is very excited

D) NM: "foreshadowing" - no future reference to this moment is possible

9

A) 2STR: "unbearable" would mean pain that cannot be withstood

B) 2STR: "chaotic" is complete confusion and disorder, not the "unmixed" (line 72) happiness that Dantes is feeling.

C) OPP: he thinks happiness changes and is unpredictable

D) ANSWER: "burdensome" = Dantes feels unworthy to be Mercedes' husband, which explains why he finds the happiness burdensome.

10

A) NI - this is the point of view of Caderousse, Dantes' friend. The correct answer should be one that explains Dantes' perspective.

B) ANSWER: "oppress" in line 64 - Dantes considers happiness to be strangely oppressive.

C) NI - Dantes thinks that men do not deserve to be so happy. However, this does not help us answer the previous question.

D) NI - Caderousse tries to cheer up his gloomy friend Dante. This is irrelevant to helping us answer the previous question.

Passage 2

11

A) NM: "Poverty" is the danger word. It is not mentioned.

B) NI: "Improve health" is the danger phrase. It's not important.

C) 2gen: "primary factors" is the danger phrase, too general. Noise is the main point.

D) ANSWER: impact of "noise exposure" on "learning environments" is the main point. (line 9-11)

12

A) NM: "conflict" is the danger word. It is not mentioned.

B) ANSWER: chronically noisy environment = "ongoing noise." negative effects on learning = "increase... educational difficulties." (line 19-21)

C) 2str:"largest sources" is the danger word. It is too extreme.

D) NI: "fail to recall or recognize" is the danger word. This is not the point of the passage.

13

A) 2gen: The statement is too general. It talks about noise exposure in general, not chronic noise exposure.

B) ANSWER: "ongoing" "educational difficulties"

C) NI: "sources" are not an important part of Q12.

D) 2sp: "deficit in memory" is the danger phrase. It is too specific.

14

A) NM: problem is not revolved around.

B) **ANSWER: focus more on "the problem" (line 23) is the right word usage.**

C) NM: there is only one problem that is centered around.

D) NM: there is only one problem that is centered around.

15

A) 2str: "permanent" is the danger word. It is too extreme.

B) NI: The paragraph is about noise intrusion, so "recognition than with recall" is the dnager word. It is not important.

C) **ANSWER: Noise intrusions = "noisy conditions" (line 53) harmful effects on learning = difficulty performing cognitive tasks (line 61)**

D) NM: "economic problems" is the danger word. It is not mentioned.

16

A) NM: literal meaning of 'pronounced'

B) NM: not related to the word.

C) NM: literal meaning of 'pronounced'

D) **ANSWER: the word is comparing recall and recognition.**

17

A) NM: Does not mention "student-generated noise."

B) 2gen: Includes too many types of noise. So it's too general.

C) NM: The lines talk about noise generated from heating and ventilation.

D) **ANSWER: "noise generated by students engaged in learning" (line 35-36) "exacerbated" (line 38)**

18

A) NM: "updated and standardized" is the danger phrase. It is not mentioned.

B) **ANSWER: understanding noise = "wider perspective" "a range of approaches" line 65-71, 80-83**

C) NI, 2str: To say that it will "remain a challenge" because the paragraph suggests solutions.

D) 2sp: "insulation" is the danger word. Too specific of a method.

19

A) OPP

B) OPP

C) **ANSWER: D,F**

D) led to 2st

20

A) OPP

B) OPP

C) OPP

D) **smallest difference. F**

21

A) NM: "hearing damage" is the danger word. It's not mentioned.

B) **ANSWER: "noise levels" and "reverberation" are in the graph.**

C) NM: "cognitive functioning" is the danger word. It's not mentioned in the graph.

D) NM: "noise leaking" is the danger word. It's not mentioned in the graph.

Passage 3

22

A) OPP: It estranges inanimate objects. so "closer to" is the danger word.

B) ANSWER: "consequences" are repercussions.

C) NM: The passage does not talk about "racist," so this is the danger word.

D) NM: "further simplified" is the danger word. it is not mentioned.

23

A) 2gen: The lines talk about the function of naming.

B) ANSWER: the lines talk about "consequences" of naming.

C) NM: using the term 'animal' is not mentioned.

D) 2sp: talks about a negative connotation, but only about 'animal,' so this is the danger word.

24

A) NM: 'self-awareness' is the danger word, which is not mentioned.

B) NM: 'human contact' is the danger word, which is not mentioned.

C) NM: 'other animals' abilities' is the danger word, which is not mentioned.

D) ANSWER; estrange = "distancing ourselves" line 46-47

25

Vocab - "guessing the word" should give you "appropriate" or "correct"

A) NM

B) NM

C) ANSWER: suitable here means appropriately.

D) NM "decourous" is an adjective related to appearance, not a method.

26

A) OPP: Kaplan does not tell whether she likes Bildungsromans, so 'dislikes' is the danger word.

B) NI: Bildungsroman has nothing to do with being 'quite skilled at writing.' This is not important.

C) ANSWER: Bildungsroman is about "growing into," which is maturing. line 98-100

D) OPP: Kaplan appreciates learning a language, so 'regrets' is the danger word.

27

A) OPP: "risk-taking" is the danger word because Bildungsromans is "safer" (line 100).

B) ANSWER: The word "transformation" appears in line 98-100.

C) NM: "curiosity" is the danger word, which is not mentioned.

D) NM: "immerse, fields" are the danger words, which are not mentioned.

28

A) NM: "irony" is the danger word. P2 has an earnest tone.

B) ANSWER: line 90-92 compare "language" to a "home."

C) NM: "jargon" is the danger word, which is not mentioned.

D) NM: past is the danger word, which is not mentioned.

29

A) ANSWER: 'implications of language' is labeling in p1 and learning a second language in p2.

B) only p2 mentions 'bilingualism' so this is the danger word.

C) only p1 talks about 'labeling' so this is the danger word.

D) NM: neither passage talks about 'creativity' so this is the danger word.

30

A) OPP: P1 does not talk about 'first-hand experiences,' so this is the danger word. P2 does not take an 'analytical' approach, s this also is a danger word.

B) NM: P1 is not related to P2. So 'critique' is the danger word.

C) ANSWER: broader impact = consequences of naming, personal context = learning a second language

D) NM: 'anticipates' is the danger word, because P1 is not related to P2.

31

A) OPP: 'overreact' is the danger word because P1 criticizes naming.

B) NM: 'multilingual' and 'creativity' are danger words because neither is dealt with in P1.

C) ANSWER: representation: self, naming

D) NM 'understanding' is the danger word. P2 talks about maturing, not understanding.

32

A) ANSWER: lines talk about the consequences of a language. P1 is about consequences of naming.

B) NM: That language is a home is not mentioned in P1.

C) NM: P1 does not talk about persona.

D) NM: P1 is not about memoir.

Passage 4

33

A) 2str: "unavoidable" is too strong of a word. So this is the danger word.

B) N: "Fuel warfare" is the danger word. Industrial-military complex does not fuel warfare between countries.

C) 2sp: "liberty, dignity, and integrity" is the nation's goal. Not related to industrial-military complex.

D) ANSWER: extensive influence = "acquisition of unwarranted influence" (line 64-67)

34

A) OPP: The hostile philosophy refers to Soviet communism, so "national" is the danger word.

B) ANSWER: line 9-13 says this is "global in scope," so it's a threat of an international rival.

C) NM: "Military" and "society" are danger words.

The threat is about ideology.

D) NM: 'Morality' is the danger word, which is not mentioned.

35

A) NM: "the Industrial Revolution" is the danger phrase. The passage talks about technological revolution, not the Industrial Revolution.

B) NM: "manipulation" is the danger word— this has not taken place.

C) **ANSWER: line 48-50 "until the latest" is synonymous to 'a recent historical development.'**

D) NM: "war and injustice" are the danger words. They are not mentioned.

36

A) NM: the lines talk about America's adventure in free government "throughout," which is the danger word. The question asks about a recent historical development.

B) NM: The lines do not specify time.

C) **ANSWER: The lines talk about "the latest" development.**

D) NI: Although the lines about a recent development, the subject of the sentence is "research," which is the danger word.

37

A) **ANSWER: The hint is earlier in the sentence, "commands our whole attention." Here, the word "absorbs" means "to engage fully," which is closest to our hint.**

B) NM: physical meaning of absorbing (liquiD)

C) NM: falls short of extremity hinted by the word "absorbs"

D) NM: means to understand or process food

38

A) NM: "engrossed in magnitude" is the danger phrase, which is not mentioned as an inclination.

B) NM: "lament" is the danger word, which is not mentioned as an inclination.

C) **ANSWER: idealistic solutions = "miraculous solution" (line 25)**

D) NM: "safety" is the danger word, which is not mentioned.

39

A) NM

B) NM

C) **ANSWER: the lines talk about people's inclination to seek ideal solutions.**

D) NM

40

A) 2str: "identify the consequence" is the danger phrase, because there is yet no consequence of an armaments industry.

B) NM: "present" is the danger word. There is no present misuse, only potential misuse of power.

C) NM: "increased government spending" is not mentioned.

D) **ANSWER: line 64 talks about "potential for the disastrous rise," which is intended to "caution against" unjustified control of the** government by the military.

41

A) physical

B) physical

C) ANSWER: "weight" here means emotional burden, which is closest to burden.

D) physical4

42

A) OPP: science is responsible for military development. (line 68-70)

B) OPP: Power and money are not a contrast. (line 74-75)

C) ANSWER: The government should prevent 'elite' from controlling public policy, protecting democracy. (line 78-83)

D) NM: 'the past' is the danger word, which is not mentioned. (line 85-88)

Passage 5

43

A) NM: "proven" is the danger word. A hypothesis is not proven.

B) ANSWER: large migrations of amphibians have been linked to large earthquakes," and this is the 'perceived connection. (line 3-7)

C) NI: 'media reports' is the danger word. Media report is not the focus of the paragraph.

D) NM: 'explain' is the danger word. The paragraph does not explain the cause of the earthquakes.

44

A) 2str: the alarm is not intended to deceive anyone, so this is too strong,

B) 2str: the alarm is neither intended to betray or trick anyone nor dangerous, so this is too strong.

C) ANSWER: media created "unnecessary anxiety," so it's clear that the alarms are 'unfounded' because there is no reason for alarm. (line 17-18)

D) NM: fictitious is another synonym of false, but it means imaginary or virtual.

45

A) NM: 'detect' is the danger word. There is no mentioning of frogs detecting signs of seismic activity.

B) OPP: 'do not migrate' is the danger word. Frog migration is a normal behavior (line 34-35)

C) ANSWER: the phrase "because of these two incidents" explain that the fears were caused by the migrations. (line 19-22)

D) NM: 'often'

46

A) NI: the lines do not explain fear.

B) ANSWER: the lines explain that frog migrations caused fears because they have preceded two earthquakes.

C) NM: The lines are not related to explaining why migrations triggered fears.

D) NI: The lines just explain migrations might be reported as "frog swarms" by media.

47

A) OPP: 'variable' means it's changeable, so it means the opposite of 'accidental.'

B) **ANSWER: it says it is variable from "year to year" (line 64), which implies that it is different every year.**

C) OPP: 'fleeting' means temporary, which does not fit in with the context.

D) OPP: 'transitory' also means temporary, which does not fit in with the context.

48

A) **ANSWER: irregular behavior should be "interpreted with caution" and "consultation with experts…is advised," which is synonymous to not simply dismissing it.**

B) NM: "emotional problems" is the danger word, which is not mentioned.

C) 2str: "immature tendencies" is the danger phrase. It is personifying frogs.

D) 2str: "continue to be" is the danger phrase because this claim is unsupported.

49

A) NM: the lines talk about the possibility of frog swarms causing unnecessary alarms.

B) NI: The lines talk about media reports of frog migrations that did not precede earthquakes.

C) NI: The lines talk about the periods in which frog migrations take place.

D) **ANSWER: the lines talk about the need to approach amphibian behavior with expert opinion.**

50

graph

A) NM

B) **ANSWER: July is the highest on the graph.**

C) NM

D) NM

51

A) NM: 'successful" is the danger word. Neither the passage nor the graph show the relationship between migratory behavior and successful reproductive seasons.

B) 2str: 'not linked to' is the danger phrase because the passage says that migration might sometimes be linked to earthquakes.

C) **ANSWER: late spring and summer = "may & july"**

D) OPP: 'unpredictable' is the danger word because the passage says that migration is predictable.

52

A) OPP: 'higher' is the danger word. It also takes place during autumn.

B) NM: during summer' is the danger word. The graph does not link migration during summer to earthquakes in summer.

C) NM: The graph only shows one year. So 'normative' is the danger word.

D) **ANSWER: The answer matches the graph.**

Part 1

SAT® Practice Test #3

Reading Test

65 MINUTES, 52 QUESTIONS

Turn to Section 1 of your answer sheet to answer the questions in this section.

DIRECTIONS

Each passage or pair of passages below is followed by a number of questions. After reading each passage or pair, choose the best answer to each question based on what is stated or implied in the passage or passages and in any accompanying graphics (such as a table or graph).

Questions 1-10 are based on the following passage.

This passage is adapted from *Treasure Island* by Robert Louis Stevenson. Originally published in 1882.

    I remember him as if it were yesterday, as he came plodding to the inn door, his sea-chest following behind him in a hand-barrow—a tall, strong, heavy,
Line man, his pigtail falling over the shoulder of his soiled
5 blue coat, his hands ragged and scarred, with black, broken nails. Then he rapped on the door, and when my father appeared, called roughly for a glass of rum. This, when it was brought to him, he drank slowly, like a connoisseur, lingering on the taste and still
10 looking about him at the cliffs and up at our signboard.
    He stayed with us then at the inn for a long while after. There were nights when he took a deal more rum and water than his head would carry; and then he
15 would sometimes sit and sing his wicked, old, wild sea-songs, minding nobody; but sometimes he would call for glasses round and force all the trembling company to listen to his stories or bear a chorus to his singing. Often I have heard the house shaking with
20 "Yo-ho-ho, and a bottle of rum," all the neighbours joining in for dear life, with the fear of death upon them, and each singing louder than the other to avoid remark. For in these fits he was the most overriding companion ever known; he would slap his hand on the
25 table for silence all round; he would fly up in a passion of anger at a question, or sometimes because none was put, and so he judged the company was not following his story. Nor would he allow anyone to leave the inn till he had drunk himself sleepy and
30 reeled off to bed. People were frightened at the time, but on looking back they rather liked it; it was a fine excitement in a quiet country life.
    He was only once crossed, and that was towards the end. Dr. Livesey came late one afternoon to see
35 the patient, took a bit of dinner from my mother, and went into the parlour to smoke a pipe until his horse should be ready. Suddenly he—the captain, that is—began to pipe up his eternal song:
        "Fifteen men on the dead man's chest—
40   Yo-ho-ho, and a bottle of rum!
        Drink and the devil had done for the rest—
        Yo-ho-ho, and a bottle of rum!"
    By this time we had all long ceased to pay any particular notice to the song; it was new, that night,
45 to nobody but Dr. Livesey, and on him I observed it did not produce an agreeable effect, for he looked up for a moment quite angrily before he went on with his talk. In the meantime, the captain gradually brightened up at his own music, and at last flapped
50 his hand upon the table before him in a way we all knew to mean silence. The voices stopped at once, all but Dr. Livesey's; he went on as before speaking clear and kind and drawing briskly at his pipe between every word or two. The captain glared at
55 him for a while, flapped his hand again, glared still harder, and at last broke out with a villainous, low oath, "Silence, there, between decks!"
    "Were you addressing me, sir?" says the doctor; and when the ruffian had told him, with another oath,

that this was so, "I have only one thing to say to you, sir," replies the doctor, "that if you keep on drinking rum, the world will soon be quit of a very dirty scoundrel!"

The doctor never so much as moved. He spoke to him as before, over his shoulder and in the same tone of voice, rather high, so that all the room might hear, but perfectly calm and steady: "If you do not put that knife this instant in your pocket, I promise, upon my honour, you shall hang at the next assizes."

Then followed a battle of looks between them, but the captain soon knuckled under, put up his weapon, and resumed his seat, grumbling like a beaten dog.

"And now, sir," continued the doctor, "since I now know there's such a fellow in my district, you may count I'll have an eye upon you day and night. I'm not a doctor only; I'm a magistrate; and if I catch a breath of complaint against you, if it's only for a piece of incivility like tonight's, I'll take effectual means to have you hunted down and routed out of this. Let that suffice."

Soon after, Dr. Livesey's horse came to the door and he rode away, but the captain held his peace that evening, and for many evenings to come.

1

Which of the following best summarizes the passage?
A) A young boy discovers that not all adults are as trustworthy as they seem.
B) An overbearing person is outmatched by a more powerful person.
C) A traumatized sailor finds companionship amongst a seaside community.
D) A pirate criminal is nearly arrested by the police that have been searching for him.

2

In line 7, "roughly" most nearly means
A) furiously.
B) agitatedly.
C) approximately.
D) coarsely.

3

Within the passage, it is most clearly implied that the majority of the people at the inn regard found the pirate captain
A) confusing.
B) formidable.
C) contemptible.
D) tedious.

4

Which choice provides the best evidence for the answer to the previous question?
A) Lines 13-16 ("There ... nobody")
B) Lines 19-23 ("Often ... remark")
C) Lines 25-28 ("he would ... story")
D) Lines 43-45 ("By ... Dr. Livesey")

5

The description of the consequences of when the pirate captain "took a deal more rum and water than his head would carry" (lines 13-14) primarily serve to
A) indicate the extremity of his dependency on alcohol.
B) explain why so many patrons of the inn found him fascinating.
C) highlight that people's reaction to him was a mixture of fear and appreciation.
D) show the impact of his violence and cruelty.

6

As used in line 33, "crossed" most nearly means
A) mixed.
B) complicated.
C) confused.
D) opposed.

7

The passage indicates that the pirate captain's antics were
A) far beyond acceptable behavior for the townspeople.
B) a source of growing fame for the inn.
C) established as routine by the time Dr. Livesey arrived.
D) the reason for Dr. Livesey's appearance at the inn.

8

As presented in the passage, Dr. Livesey is best described as
A) quiet but intimidating.
B) civil but arrogant.
C) well-groomed but vain.
D) wealthy but despised.

9

Which choice provides the best evidence for the answer to the previous question?
A) Lines 51-54 ("The voices ... two")
B) Lines 60-63 ("I have ... scoundrel")
C) Lines 70-72 ("Then ... dog")
D) Lines 76-80 ("I'm ... suffice")

10

One implied result of the confrontation between the pirate captain and Dr. Livesey was that the pirate was
A) publicly executed.
B) eventually exiled.
C) subsequently arrested.
D) temporarily subdued.

Questions 11-20 are based on the following passage and supplementary materials.

This passage is adapted from "Alcohol-Induced Blackout" by Lee H, Roh S, Kim DJ, 2009. Published in the International Journal of Environmental Research and Public Health.

Alcohol is a threat to global health, accounting for 4% of the global health burden, a proportion that is comparable to tobacco and hypertension. Dysfunctions of multiple organ systems brought on by chronic
[5] alcohol use, including the brain, have long been the focus of medical concern, and are well documented in the public health literature. Nevertheless, alcohol continues to be a part of human culture. Acute effects of alcohol intoxication are a common—often
[10] voluntary—experience and not necessarily considered a problem in itself. The alcoholic blackout, however, is one phenomenon of acute alcohol intoxication that merits special attention.

An alcoholic blackout is amnesia for the events of
[15] any part of a drinking episode without loss of consciousness. It is characterized by memory impairment during intoxication in the relative absence of other skill deficits. It is not to be confused with 'passing out.' Early documentation from Alcoholics
[20] Anonymous describes a variety of blackout behavior, which includes driving for long distances or carrying on apparently normal conversations at parties. Subjects often report waking in strange places without any memory of how they got there. Criminal acts including
[25] murder, have been reported. Some have criticized these extremes, stating that such behavior is "exaggerated" and a form of "selective memory or denial" to avoid guilt and confrontation over antisocial behavior brought on by drinking. Regardless, selective impairment of
[30] memory definitively occurs during an alcohol-induced blackout.

A high frequency and volume of alcohol use is the single factor most closely related to experiencing blackouts. In contrast to the older misconception that
[35] blackouts are an unlikely consequence of heavy drinking in nonalcoholics, anyone who drinks too much and too fast may experience a blackout. A survey of 2,076 Finnish males concluded that 35% experienced at least one blackout in the year before
[40] the survey. Cultural and socioeconomic backgrounds are associated factors. In a separate survey of 772 undergraduates, approximately one-half of those that had ever consumed alcohol reported experiencing at least one blackout during their lives, and 40%
[45] experienced one the year before the survey.

However, in a four year follow up of young blackout drinkers, only 32% of respondents that were experiencing blackouts in the initial survey continued to experience them four years later. Alcoholic
[50] blackouts in this group appeared to have resolved spontaneously when the subjects graduated college, got married, or successfully entered the adult workforce. Spontaneous resolution of blackout drinking appears to result from an interaction between informal support
[55] and objective social conditions such as full-time employment and a positive financial situation. To a certain extent, life transitional changes such as assuming adult roles appear to be a strong influence on the process of disengagement from problem
[60] drinking. Those who continued to experience blackouts after four years were male, comparatively young, unmarried, and with a lower socioeconomic status. Finally, the most salient predictor of chronic blackout drinking was the number of alcoholic relatives.

[65] Although the alcohol-induced blackout itself may not be an indicator of progressive alcohol dependence, the way in which an individual views the experience of a blackout may be influential in determining future drinking behavior. One's drinking experience should
[70] play a role in determining one's alcohol expectancy, but limited recall of events associated with intoxication may confuse one's bases for outcome expectancies. Alcohol's initial effects are euphoria, which is then followed by more sedative effects.

[75] Blackouts are associated with rising BAC, and recall of a drinking episode may reflect the initial positive effects better than the later negative effects. A rapid rate of increase in blood alcohol concentration (BAC) is most consistently associated
[80] with the occurrence of an alcoholic blackout. Therefore, gulping drinks, drinking on an empty stomach, or drinking liquor (opposed to beer) are risk factors of an alcoholic blackout. However, not all subjects who drink rapidly and excessively experience
[85] blackouts, suggesting that there are individuals that are genetically more vulnerable to alcohol-induced memory impairment.

In order to prevent alcohol-induced blackouts, the following is recommended: drink alcohol slowly, drink
90 moderately, drink infrequently, drink with side dishes, and abstinence or moderation in drinking is especially important in high-risk groups, that is, persons with a large number of alcoholic relatives. Since alcoholic blackouts occur early in the course of disease and the
95 blackout itself may act to facilitate problematic drinking resulting in another blackout, psychoeducation targeting episodes of alcoholic blackouts may be effective in preventing further episodes and the evolution to full-blown alcoholism.

11

Which choice best represents the relationship between alcoholism and blackouts as presented in the passage?
A) Blackouts are not limited only to alcoholics, but experiencing blackouts may encourage alcoholism.
B) Recent research suggests a direct link between experiencing blackouts and the development of alcoholism.
C) Blackouts pose little to no risk of promoting the development of alcoholism when compared to one's genetic history.
D) More research must be conducted before any link between the two can be confirmed.

12

Which of the following best represents an underlying assumption of the passage in its discussion of research into alcohol related blackouts?
A) People will continue to drink alcohol, so it is important to understand the risks of intoxication.
B) The public must be convinced of the dangers of blackouts in order to prevent alcohol abuse.
C) Widespread misconceptions about the dangers of alcohol abuse lead to death and disease in the public.
D) The amount of existing research is so inconclusive and conflicting that few conclusions can be drawn.

13

Which choice provides the best evidence for the answer to the previous question?
A) Lines 1-3 ("Alcohol ... hypertension")
B) Lines 3-7 ("Dysfunctions ... literature")
C) Lines 7-13 ("Nevertheless ... attention")
D) Lines 14-18 ("An alcoholic ... deficits")

14

In line 22, "apparently" most nearly means
A) obviously.
B) probably.
C) allegedly.
D) absolutely.

15

Reference to those who have "criticized these extremes" (lines 25-26) primarily serves to
A) raise awareness of forces working to undermine efforts to improve public health.
B) highlight that in cases involving the most severe consequences, blackouts might not be the only factor involved in the outcome.
C) anticipate and refute counterarguments from those on the other side of a controversial topic.
D) concede that some aspects of the results of research into blackouts and alcoholism might be seen as objectionable by the public.

16

According to the research discussed in the fourth paragraph (lines 46-64), the biggest risk factor for an alcohol-induced blackout was
A) gender.
B) education level.
C) a personal history of alcoholism.
D) a family history of alcoholism.

17

Which of the following best represents the link between blackouts and alcoholism, according to the passage?
A) The physical effects of alcoholism reorient brain chemistry to such an extent that blackouts increase in frequency.
B) Memory loss associated with blackouts prevents subjects from remembering the negative effects of alcohol consumption.
C) Blackouts lead to increased academic and professional failure, at which point subjects become more susceptible to alcoholism.
D) Trauma sustained from family members suffering blackouts resulting from alcoholism in turn promotes alcoholism in the subjects themselves.

18

In line 76, "recall" most nearly means
A) recollection.
B) cancellation.
C) suspension.
D) introspection.

20

The passage implies that which of the following would be the most effective method of preventing blackouts?
A) People should drink carefully, with the knowledge that there is no way to be sure of preventing blackouts.
B) People should match their level of consumption to their level of academic or personal success.
C) People with a family history of alcoholism should abstain from drinking.
D) People must be aware of their family history and control their consumption.

20

Which choice provides the best evidence for the answer to the previous question?
A) Lines 29-31 ("Regardless ... blackout")
B) Lines 49-52 ("Alcoholic blackouts ... workforce")
C) Lines 83-87 ("However ... impairment")
D) Lines 88-93 ("In order ... relatives")

Questions 21-31 are based on the following passage.

This passage is adapted from "High status males invest more than high status females in lower status same-sex collaborators" by Henry Markovits, Evelyne Gauthier, Emilie Gagonon-St-Pierre, and Joyce F. Bensenson, 2017.

If resources are limited in nature, why do people cooperate? More specifically, why do people cooperate with people who don't share their genes? Are there any differences in this behavior among various types of people and the permutations of how they might interact? Cooperation between unrelated individuals, which cannot be explained by kin selection, has generated intense interest. Utilizing computational models and economic games, researchers across many diverse fields have investigated the reasons individuals choose to cooperate and share rewards with unrelated individuals.

Research on non-human primates in natural and captive settings has identified several factors that influence cooperation: dominance status, kinship, sex, age, and friendship and the social structure of the species. Computer simulations and simple economic games of human cooperation however rarely incorporate these factors. Only sex has been extensively studied in economic games, and no consistent sex differences in cooperation have been identified. Recent studies have attempted to investigate the interaction between sex and status, with the hypothesis high-ranked males will be more generous when sharing a reward after cooperation than high-ranked females.

There is evidence from a variety of sources that status has an effect on cooperative behavior. In non-human primates, when individuals cannot obtain a reward on their own, they typically choose one other dominant individual with whom to cooperate. For example, in chimpanzees, one of humans' closest living genetic relatives, community males interact in hierarchical groups. When too many females are present for the alpha to guard, cooperative mate guarding followed by sharing matings typically occurs between the alpha male and the second ranked male. High-ranked males also cooperate with lower-ranked males in exchange for coalitional support in agonistic encounters or more generally to maintain their status. Across primate species, cooperation and reward sharing most frequently occur between two individuals, and between the alpha and other higher-ranked individuals. Human behavioral studies have shown that only individuals who are not strong enough to win a reward on their own chose to cooperate. In addition, when given a choice, individuals chose to cooperate with a single higher status individual. Thus, both nonhuman primates and humans choose coalitional partners in order to maximize the probability of obtaining a reward.

Critically, among humans, there is clear evidence that sex and social structure interact. Within a group, males typically organize themselves hierarchically beginning in childhood. Similarly to chimpanzee males, much human male competition occurs between competing groups, which share a dominance hierarchy controlled by high status individuals. This suggests that high status males should place a greater value on cooperative partners than would be expected solely by their objective value. By contrast, human females are more likely to enter into exclusive two-person relationships which are more stable when partners are of equal rank.

Sex-based differences do not end there. Evidence shows that human males are more likely than high status females to cooperate with lower status same-sex individuals. Specifically, cooperation between professors in the same department on a joint publication was found to be more common between higher and lower status men than between higher and lower status women. In contrast, high status male and female professors were just as likely to cooperate with same-sex individuals of identical high status. Other studies suggest that high-ranked females and males interact differently in cooperative settings, with high status male classmates interacting more equally with unrelated same-sex classmates than high status females both in early childhood, and in middle childhood. Several studies additionally demonstrate that compared with higher-status women, higher-status men perceive lower-status same-sex peers more positively.

Most companies also have clear hierarchical structures, with institutionalized status markers. Recent studies show that high status males are more willing to forgo some of the advantages of status in order to reward collaborators, which would have the associated effect of increasing the bonding of the latter to the group led by the high status male.

Coupled with the increased tendency of high status
90 males to actually cooperate with lower status peers,
this implies that males have some clear intuitions
that lead to an emphasis on group interactions,
something that is particularly important for
95 advancement within a modern corporate structure.

The current results conform closely to the
theoretical prediction that the structural properties of
human females' and males' relationships facilitate
different types of investment. If this interpretation is
100 correct, then promoting group identity, and reducing
the intense focus on one individual at a time, could
encourage more high-ranked females to invest in
their lower-ranked peers. Given the recent increase in
public awareness of the struggles of women in the
105 workplace, such information might serve as another
tool to make the career ladder more equitable for
women to climb.

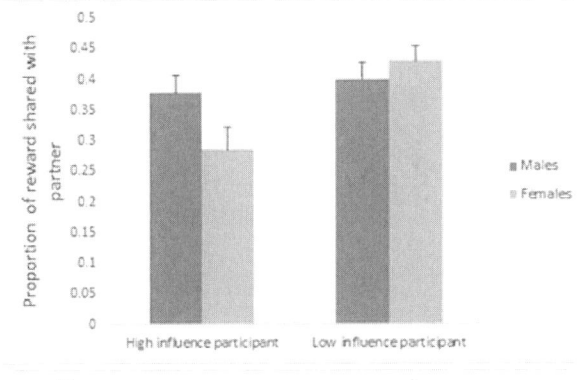

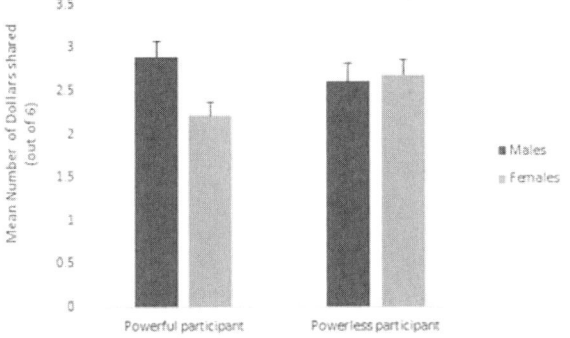

Figures adapted from "High status males invest more than high status females in lower status same-sex collaborators" by Henry Markovits, Evelyne Gauthier, Emilie Gagonon-St-Pierre, and Joyce F. Bensenson, 2017.

21

What role does the second paragraph (lines 13-26) serve in the context of the passage as a whole?
A) It outlines the limitations of existing research and proposes specific methods for surpassing them.
B) It elaborates on the points made in the first paragraph with the intention of clarifying confusing terms.
C) It presents a hypothesis as a possible answer to questions introduced earlier in the passage.
D) It proposes a new way of thinking about the topic in order to motivate researchers to pursue new lines of thinking.

22

In line 8, "intense" most nearly means
A) excessive.
B) fierce.
C) great.
D) sharp.

23

Which of the following does the author explicitly cite as a reason for a dominant chimpanzee to share rewards with a lower status male?
A) Managing social relationships
B) Redistributing food supply
C) Promoting genetic diversity
D) Limiting group size

24

Which choice provides the best evidence for the answer to the previous question?
A) Lines 13-17 ("Research ... species")
B) Lines 22-26 ("Recent ... females")
C) Lines 34-37 ("When ... male")
D) Lines 41-43 ("Across ... individuals")

25

The primary idea of the fifth paragraph (lines 65-81) is that
A) Men are more likely than women to share rewards with same-sex colleagues of lower status.
B) Men and women show no differences in the way they perceive same-sex colleagues of lower status.
C) Both men and women of high status are likely to share rewards with colleagues of either equal or lower status.
D) Men prefer to work with colleagues of lower status while women prefer to work with peers.

26

Which choice provides the best evidence for the answer to the previous question?
A) Line 65 ("Sex-based ... there")
B) Lines 65-68 ("Evidence ... individuals")
C) Lines 72-74 ("In contrast ... status")
D) Lines 80-82 ("Several ... positively")

27

In line 102, "invest in" most nearly means
A) supply.
B) establish.
C) bankroll.
D) promote.

28

Which choice best supports the idea that current workplace dynamics among women might be hindering their professional success?
A) Lines 84-89 ("Recent ... male")
B) Lines 96-99 ("The current ... investment")
C) Lines 99-103 ("If this ... peers")
D) Lines 103-107 ("Given ... climb")

29

Which choice is the correct interpretation of the data in the first figure?
A) High influence males and low influence females share the highest proportion of their rewards.
B) Low influence participants share more of their reward on average than high influence participants.
C) High influence females are the least likely to cooperate with low influence females in the workplace.
D) Low influence males are equally as likely as high influence males to share their rewards.

30

What best describes the relationship between the first and second figure?

A) Figure 2 presents data that directly refutes the data in Figure 1.
B) Figure 2 presents data related to human men and women while Figure 1 deals with all primates.
C) Figure 2 presents data from a specific circumstance that corroborate the general data in Figure 1.
D) Figure 2 presents data that strongly undermine the significance of the data in Figure 1.

Questions 31-41 are based on the following passages.

Passage 1 is adapted from *Emile* by Jean Jacques Rousseau, 1762. Passage 2 is adapted from *Democracy and Education* by John Dewey, 1914.

Passage 1

God makes all things good; man meddles with them and they become evil. He forces one soil to yield the products of another, one tree to bear another's fruit. He mutilates his dog, his horse, and
[5] his slave. He destroys and defaces all things; he loves all that is deformed and monstrous; he will have nothing as nature made it, not even man himself, who must learn his paces like a saddle-horse, and be shaped to his master's taste like the trees in
[10] his garden.

We are born sensitive and from our birth onwards we are affected in various ways by our environment. As soon as we become conscious of our sensations we tend to seek or shun the things that cause them,
[15] at first because they are pleasant or unpleasant, then because they suit us or not, and at last because of judgments formed by means of the ideas of happiness and goodness which reason gives us. These tendencies gain strength and permanence with the
[20] growth of reason, but hindered by our habits they are more or less warped by our prejudices. Before this change they are what I call Nature within us.

Everything should therefore be brought into harmony with these natural tendencies, and that might
[25] well be if our three modes of education merely differed from one another; but what can be done when they conflict, when instead of training man for himself you try to train him for others? Harmony becomes impossible. Forced to combat either nature
[30] or society, you must make your choice between the man and the citizen, you cannot train both.
The public institute does not and cannot exist, for there is neither country nor patriot. The very words should be struck out of our language.

[35] I do not consider our ridiculous colleges as public institutes, nor do I include under this head a fashionable education, for this education facing two ways at once achieves nothing. It is only fit to turn out hypocrites, always professing to live for others,
[40] while thinking of themselves alone. These professions, however, deceive no one, for every one has his share in them; they are so much labour wasted. Our inner conflicts are caused by these contradictions. Drawn this way by nature and that way by man, compelled
[45] to yield to both forces, we make a compromise and reach neither goal. We go through life, struggling and hesitating, and die before we have found peace, useless alike to ourselves and to others.

Passage 2

Observation of natural tendencies is difficult
[50] under conditions of restraint. They show themselves most readily in a child's spontaneous sayings and doings,—that is, in those he engages in when not put at set tasks and when not aware of being under observation. It does not follow that these tendencies
[55] are all desirable because they are natural; but it does follow that since they are there, they are operative and must be taken account of. We must see to it that the desirable ones have an environment which keeps them active, and that their activity shall
[60] control the direction the others take and thereby induce the disuse of the latter because they lead to nothing. At all events, adults too easily assume their own habits and wishes as standards, and regard all deviations of children's impulses as evils to be
[65] eliminated. That artificiality against which the conception of following nature is so largely a protest, is the outcome of attempts to force children directly into the mold of grown-up standards.

The early history of the idea of following nature
[70] combined two factors which had no inherent connection with one another. Before the time of Rousseau, educational reformers had been inclined to urge the importance of education by ascribing practically unlimited power to it. All the differences
[75] between peoples and between classes and persons among the same people were said to be due to differences of training, of exercise, and practice. Originally, mind, reason, and understanding were, for all practical purposes, the same in all. This essential
[80] identity of mind meant the essential equality of all and the possibility of bringing them all to the same level. Those against this view, as Rousseau was, claimed that the doctrine of accord with nature meant a much less formal and abstract view of mind
[85] and its powers than previously argued. It substituted specific instincts and impulses and physiological capacities that differ from individual to individual for the abstract, universal faculties of discernment, memory, and generalization. Upon this side, the

doctrine of educative accord with nature has been
supported by the development of modern biology,
physiology, and psychology. This means, in effect,
that great as is the significance of nurture, of
transformation through direct educational effort,
nature, or unlearned capacity, affords the foundation
and ultimate resources for such nurture.

On the other hand, the doctrine of following
nature was a political dogma. It meant a rebellion
against existing social institutions, customs, and
ideals. Rousseau's statement that everything is good
as it comes from the hands of the Creator has its
signification only in its contrast with the concluding
part of the same sentence: "Everything degenerates in
the hands of man." It is upon this conception of the
artificial and harmful character of organized social
life as it now exists that he rested the notion that
nature not merely furnishes prime forces which
initiate growth but also its plan and goal. That evil
institutions and customs work almost automatically to
give a wrong education which the most careful
schooling cannot offset is true enough; but the
conclusion is not to educate apart from that
environment, but rather to provide an environment in
which native powers will be put to better uses.

31

In line 3, "bear" most nearly means
A) produce.
B) uphold.
C) allow.
D) take.

32

It can be inferred that the author of Passage 1 believes that society
A) fails to produce useful citizens due to the interference of natural human responses.
B) is an imperfect but ultimately useful tool for improving people's lives.
C) will eventually improve itself only by recognizing that what is natural is good.
D) is an artificial construct that serves no useful purpose.

33

Which choice provides the best evidence for the answer to the previous question?
A) Lines 5-10 ("He ... garden")
B) Lines 13-14 ("As soon ... cause them")
C) Lines 32-34 ("The public ... language")
D) Lines 42-43 ("Our ... contradictions")

34

According to the author of Passage 2, the natural impulses of humanity are
A) wholly perfect, and the interference of society only corrupts them.
B) one of many sources from which to draw guidelines for education.
C) irrelevant to the needs of society.
D) not necessarily good, but also must not be ignored in education.

35

In line 73, "urge" most nearly means
A) advocate.
B) plead.
C) force.
D) desire.

36

In Passage 2, the author claims that dissatisfaction with society is a result of
A) artificial divisions resulting from long periods of separation from nature.
B) inequalities that exist among different classes.
C) children being compelled by adults to conform with adult values.
D) adults weakening and overriding the inherent beauty of nature.

37

Which choice provides the best evidence for the answer to the previous question?
A) Lines 50-54 ("They ... observation")
B) Lines 65-68 ("That ... standards")
C) Lines 69-71 ("The early ... another")
D) Lines 78-79 ("Originally ... all")

38

In lines 100-104, the author of Passage 2 refers specifically to statements made by the author of Passage 1 in order to
A) point out a logical absurdity that the author Passage 1 failed to note.
B) lament the failures of policy that have resulted from recommendations in Passage 1.
C) highlight the differences he has with the author Passage 1 on what to do about the evils of society.
D) reaffirm the conclusions of the author of Passage 1, but also rebuke him for not going far enough.

39

Which of the following best describes the overall relationship between Passage 1 and Passage 2?
A) Passage 2 elaborates upon concepts introduced in the arguments of Passage 1.
B) Passage 2 concedes certain benefits of, but ultimately rejects the proposals of Passage 1.
C) Passage 2 explores but fails to find redeeming value in the point of view of Passage 1.
D) Passage 2 lists a number of ways in which society might adopt programs that follow the values of Passage 1.

40

The authors of both passages would most likely agree with which of the following?

A) The only reasonable response to an unjust society is to reject it completely.
B) Public education can and must make room for what is natural in each individual.
C) Our individual natures often develop in conflict with what society requires of us.
D) Each individual is born with equal ability, and later differences result only from unequal education.

41

The author of Passage 1 would mostly likely view the conclusion in the final sentence (lines 108-114) of Passage 2 as

A) idealistic.
B) implausible.
C) necessary.
D) detestable.

Questions 42-52 are based on the following passage and supplementary material.

This passage is excerpt from "Alternative Resources for Renewable Energy: piezoelectric and Photovoltaic Smart Structure" by D. Vatansever, E. Siores and T. Shah, 2012.

Energy harvesting is the process of extracting, converting, and storing energy from the environment that can also be described as a response of smart
Line materials when they are subjected to an external
5 stimulus such as pressure, vibrations, motion, and temperature emanating from wind, rain, waves, tides, light and so on. The efficiency of devices in capturing trace amounts of energy from the environment and transforming it into electrical energy
10 has increased with the development of new materials and techniques. This has sparked interest in the engineering community to seek out applications that utilize energy harvesting technologies for power generation. Technologies related to photovoltaic and
15 piezoelectric materials are among the most promising in this regard.

Since the sun is the most abundant renewable energy source in the world and the solar energy the earth receives in an hour is greater than the energy
20 consumed in a year, photovoltaic (solar) materials are one of the most significant alternative energy harvesters. The proportion of sunlight energy is significant for the conversion efficiency of a PV cell which converts sunlight energy to electrical energy.
25 The efficiency of PV energy is important to make PV energy competitive with more traditional sources of energy, such as fossil fuels. For comparison, the earliest PV devices converted about 1%-2% of sunlight energy into electric energy. Today, it is
30 likely to produce photovoltaic structures made of pure silicon with 24.7% efficiency. However, due to the rigidity of silicon based solar cells and pursuit of lightweight and flexible photovoltaic materials for curved structures, applications are limited.

35 Piezoelectric effect is a unique property that allows materials to convert mechanical energy to electrical energy and conversely, electrical energy to mechanical energy. The stimuli for piezoelectric materials can be human walking, wind, rain, tide,
40 ocean waves, or any physical motion. Piezoelectric behaviour was first found in some crystals. In 1817 Charles Coulomb first theorized that electricity might be produced through the application of pressure to
45 certain types of materials. However, it was only a notion until the actual discovery of the "direct-piezoelectric phenomenon" on quartz by Pierre and Jacque Curie. They placed weights on the crystals and detected some charges on the surface
50 and also observed that the magnitude of detected charge was proportional to the applied weight.

Renewable energy sources are endless but not available at all times at a given location. For instance, the electrical energy generation by a
55 photovoltaic material is dependent on the light density and the number of photons absorbed by the photoactive layer. If the solar radiation is scarce in a region, for example on a cloudy day, the electrical energy generation will be affected. If flexible solar
60 cells are coupled with flexible piezoelectric materials in a combined structure, then the hybrid structure can generate energy from solar radiation as well as mechanical energy, such as wind, rainfall, waves etc.

A novel technology, hybrid piezoelectric-
65 photovoltaic material (HPP), has been developed by that integrates piezoelectric polymer substrate and photovoltaic coating system to create a film or a fibre structure which is able to transform both mechanical energy (through piezoelectricity) and light
70 energy (through an organic photovoltaic covering). Since the photovoltaic material system is organically produced, the cost associated with the whole structure is encouragingly less than silicon based photovoltaic. The resultant material system is flexible
75 and can be incorporated in textiles for a wide variety of applications, under different environments on earth, underwater and, even more thrillingly, space.

The HPP materials are able to produce electrical
80 energy from the environment and provide almost uninterrupted energy generation to power small electronic devices. The flexible HPP structure can be part of any material such as sail, window curtain, tent etc. to generate renewable energy even in the
85 absence of sunlight. One possible configuration for land-based applications of hybrid fibre is a pine tree like structure where the needles are made of HPP fibres. Such a structure may replace the conventional photovoltaic parks that require large panels and sun

tracking devices to operate. The surface area that
fibres provide is substantially more compared to the
solar panels, thus they may be able to generate more
energy in a confined area. The tree structure also
costs less to manufacture and can harvest energy not
only through the photovoltaic but also through the
piezoelectric material. Furthermore, the aesthetic
aspects of parks incorporating them cannot be
overstated. Once flexible fibres are incorporated in
textile structures, a plethora of opportunities exist,
limited only by the imagination.

Piezoelectric Material	BaTiO$_3$	PZT	PVDF
Density	5.7 10^{3}kg/m^3	7.5 10^{3}kg/m^3	1.78 10^{3}kg/m^3
Resistance	1,700 ε/ε$_0$	1,200 ε/ε$_0$	12 ε/ε$_0$
Piezoelectric Efficiency	78 10^{-12}C/N	110 10^{-12}C/N	23 10^{-12}C/N
Voltage	5 10^{-3}Vm/N	10 10^{-3}Vm/N	216 10^{-3}Vm/N

Figures adapted from *Alternative Resources for Renewable Energy: piezoelectric and Photovoltaic Smart Structure*, D. Vatansever, E. Siores and T. Shah, 2012.

42

How do the words "novel," "encouragingly," and "thrillingly" (lines 64-78) work to establish the tone of the fifth paragraph?

A) They create an exaggerated tone that undermines the authors' claims of neutrality toward renewable energy.
B) They create a tone of mixed emotion that makes clear the authors have reservations about the viability of HPP materials.
C) They create an ironic tone that makes clear the authors intended meaning is actually the opposite of what is written.
D) They create an optimistic tone that indicates the possibility of bias on the part of the author regarding HPP materials.

43

In lines 14-16, the authors claim that a certain technology is "the most promising" in regards to energy generation. According to the passage, why is this the case?

A) A utilization of the technology to its full potential could provide energy generation in a diverse number of situations.
B) The use of this technology will overcome limitations to existing photovoltaic technology and make it the primary energy source of civilization.
C) The technologies previously associated with piezoelectric phenomenon have long been proven to be too expensive for practical applications.
D) Neither photovoltaic nor piezoelectric phenomenon generate enough electricity to be practical when they are forced to interact with one another.

44

Which choice provides the best evidence for the answer to the previous question?
A) Lines 20-22 ("photovoltaic ... harvesters")
B) Lines 38-41 ("The stimuli ... crystals")
C) Lines 41-45 ("In 1817 ... materials")
D) Lines 98-100 ("Once ... imagination")

45

The authors most strongly suggest which of the following regarding the development of photovoltaic technology?
A) It is still too inflexible to be a viable alternative to fossil fuels.
B) It will eventually be able to turn one hour of sunlight into a year's worth of energy.
C) It has dramatically increased in efficiency over time.
D) Increases in efficiency will eventually make it competitive with fossil fuels.

46

Which choice provides the best evidence for the answer to the previous question?
A) Lines 17-20 ("Since ... year")
B) Lines 22-28 ("The proportion ... fuels")
C) Lines 28-32 ("For ... efficiency")
D) Lines 32-35 ("However ... limited")

47

As used in line 46, "notion" most nearly means
A) impulse.
B) clue.
C) image.
D) proposition.

48

The main purpose of the final paragraph (lines 79-100) is to
A) speculate on the possible uses of HPP technology once it becomes more fully developed.
B) imagine the aesthetic benefits to society of public parks that utilize fully realized HPP technology.
C) warn against the dangers of using HPP technology to replace natural flora with hybrid electricity generating devices.
D) predict a future in which the majority of human electrical demand is met by artificial trees crafted from HPP materials.

49

An unstated assumption made by the authors about energy generation is that
A) current photovoltaic and piezoelectric technologies are not developed enough to pose a legitimate challenge to fossil fuels.
B) the capture of trace amounts of electricity from the environment is intriguing to engineers.
C) renewable energy sources are unreliable in the amount of electricity they produce.
D) alternatives to existing electricity generation methods are necessary.

50

Based on data in the table, what is the resistance rate of the piezoelectric material with the greatest piezoelectric efficiency?

A) 110 10-12 C/N
B) 1,700 $\varepsilon/\varepsilon_0$
C) 1,200 $\varepsilon/\varepsilon_0$
D) 12 $\varepsilon/\varepsilon_0$

51

Based on data in the table, which piezoelectric material has both the lowest density and the highest voltage?

A) $BaTiO_3$
B) PZT
C) PVDF
D) This information cannot be determined from the table.

52

Do the data in the table provide support for the author's claim in line 48-51 about the nature of the piezoelectric phenomena?

A) No, because the table provides insufficient data points to establish a confident link between weight and charge.
B) No, because the table does not provide any information establishing a link between weight and charge.
C) Yes, because the density and voltage of the materials in question is sufficient to establish a link between weight and charge.
D) Yes, because the data on resistance in the table clearly indicates "direct-piezoelectric phenomenon."

STOP

If you finish before time is called, you may check your work on this section only.

Do not turn to any other section.

Part 1

Practice Test 3:
Answer Key and Explanations

Reading Test 3 Answer Key

Reading Test 3	
Question	Answer
1	B
2	D
3	B
4	B
5	C
6	D
7	C
8	A
9	C
10	D
11	A
12	A
13	C
14	C
15	B
16	D
17	B
18	A
19	D
20	D
21	C
22	C
23	A
24	C
25	A
26	B

Reading Test 3	
Question	Answer
27	D
28	D
29	B
30	C
31	A
32	D
33	C
34	D
35	A
36	C
37	B
38	C
39	D
40	C
41	B
42	D
43	A
44	D
45	C
46	C
47	D
48	A
49	D
50	C
51	C
52	B

*For self-scoring assessment tables, please turn to page 189.

Passage 1

1

A) NM, NI: "trustworthy" is the danger word, it is not mentioned. And also not important what "young boy" thinks.

B) **ANSWER: "Overbearing person" is the captain, and "a more powerful person" Dr. Livesey. The passage talks about the tension between the two and the eventual defeat of the captain.**

C) NM: "traumatized" is the danger word. It is not mentioned.

D) NM: "have been searching for him" is the danger word. Dr. Livesey threatens to tell the police, but police hasn't been looking for the captain.

2

A) 2str: "furiously" is too strong because it refers to anger, and we don't know if the captain is angry when knocking on the door.

B) 2str: "agitatedly" is also too strong because it refers to emotion.

C) NM: "Approximately" is used when referring to a number.

D) **ANSWER: "Coarsely" describes the physical manner in which the captain knocks the door.**

3

A) OPP: "confusing" is not correct because people are aware of the captains' behavioral patterns (line 43)

B) **ANSWER: the captain frightens people.**

C) 2str: Contemptible is too strong of a word because people rather liked him. (line 31)

D) OPP: The captain is scary—can't be boring.

4

A) NM: the line evidence talks about the captain's actions, not people's reactions.

B) **ANSWER: "joining in for dear life" shows that people are scared of the captain, therefore shows that they think of him as "formidable"**

C) NM: the lines talk about the captain's actions.

D) NI: does not talk about the captain, talks about the song. And Dr. Livesey's presence.

5

A) 2str: "extremity" is the danger word. The captain drinks that much only on some nights.

B) NM: "fascinating" is the danger word. The crowd is scared of him.

C) **ANSWER: People are scared, but they also have fun. (line 20-22, 30-32)**

D) 2str: "violence" and "cruelty" are too strong because people are appreciate him.

6

A) a person cannot be "mixed." Synonym of crossed that refers to physical quality

B) "Complicated" is a state of being, but the word refers to an occasion.

C) The captain is clearly not "confused," he is angry

D) **ANSWER: "once crossed" refers to the adversarial encounter between Dr. Livesey and the captain.**

7

A) 2str: "far beyond acceptable" is too strong. People rather liked him. (line 30-32)

B) NM: "fame" is the danger word, not mentioned.

C) ANSWER: "routine" = line 43-45 shows that only Dr. Livesey is not familiar with his antics.

D) NM: Dr. Livesey came to see the patient. (line 34-35)

8

A) ANSWER: quiet = "a battle of looks" (line 70). Intimidating = "the captain soon knuckled under" (line 71)

B) NM: "arrogant" is the danger word; the doctor does not show off (he threatens).

C) NM: "well-groomed" and "vain" refer to physical appearance, which is not mentioned.

D) NM: "wealthy" and "despised" are not mentioned.

9

A) NM: a comparison between Dr. Livesey's reaction and the people's reaction to the captain's exclamation.

B) NM: Dr. Livesey is threatening the captain, but at this point we don't know if he is intimidating.

C) ANSWER: he makes the captain "knuckle under" just by looking at him (without talking).

D) again, Dr. Livesey is threatening the captain, but he is not quiet.

10

A) 2str: Dr. Livesey threatens to have him hanged, but the captain is not actually hanged yet.

B) 2str: the captain just grows quiet; he is not exiled.

C) 2str: Dr. Livesy threatens to call the police, but not yet.

D) ANSWER: the captain is subdued ("held his peace...for many evenings to come." line 82-83).

Passage 2

11

A) ANSWER: not limited only alcoholics (line 7-11) may encourage alcoholism (line 34-37)

B) 2str: "direct link" is the danger word, blackouts may or may not lead to alcoholism.

C) 2str: "little to no risk" is the danger word. Although one's genetic history is important, blackouts also influence alcoholism (line 65-69)

D) 2str: "any link" is the danger word because the passage talks about the link between blackouts and alcoholism.

12

A) ANSWER: people will continue to drink alcohol (line 7-8), so it is important to understand the risks of intoxication (line 11-13)

B) NM, 2str: "the public" is the danger word. "must be" is too strong of a word.

C) NM, 2str: "death and disease" is the danger word. They are not mentioned/too strong.

D) 2str: "so inconclusive and conflicting" are the danger phrase, the passage clearly states how to prevent alcoholism.

13

A) NM: "global health burden" is not mentioned.

B) NM, 2sp: "dysfunctions of organ systems" is not mentioned. Too specific.

C) ANSWER: "part of human culture" = people will continue to drink, 'alcohol intoxication that merits special attention' = important to understand the risk

D) NM: the lines just explains the definition of "blackout."

14

A) 2str: "subjects" claim that they were carrying out normal conversations, but the claim is not obvious.

B) NM: no clue whether the conversations were normal or not.

C) ANSWER: the subjects claim that they were having normal conversations, and allegedly means "asserted to be true"

D) 2str: that the subjects were having normal conversation is not obvious.

15

A) 2gen, NM: "public health" is the danger word. It's too broad of a subject. "Forces working to undermine efforts" have not been mentioned.

B) ANSWER: "selective memory or denial" is mentioned right after to explain another factor involved in severe consequences. (line 27-29)

C) 2str: people who criticize extreme behaviors are not "on the other side of a controversial topic."

The author also does not argue against this claim.

D) NM: "Objectionable by the public" is the danger phrase. How the public views research on alcoholism is not mentioned.

16

A) NI: although many who experienced blackout were "male," not the most important factor. (line 61)

B) NI: the author mentions "college" to discuss a shift in lifestyle, not education level. (line 51)

C) OPP: "life transitional changes" tend to influence "disengagement" from alcoholism. (line 56-60)

D) ANSWER: "the most salient predictor" (line 63-64) = the biggest risk factor. "the number of alcoholic relatives" = a family history of alcoholism.

17

A) NM, 2str: "Reorient brain chemistry" is the danger phrase. This is not mentioned. "to such an extent" is too extreme.

B) ANSWER: Memory loss associated with blackouts = "limited recall if events associated with intoxication (line 71-72)", prevents subjects from remembering the negative effects of alcohol consumption = "may confuse one's bases for outcome expectancies. Alcohol's initial effects are euphoria (line 72-73)".

C) NM: "increased academic and professional failure" are the danger words, they are not mentioned.

D) NM: "trauma sustained from family members suffering blackouts" are not mentioned.

18

A) **ANSWER: the context shows recall means "remembering" a drinking episode.**

B) OPP: remembering is not cancelling.

C) OPP: suspension here means holding up.

D) NM: introspection means looking into oneself.

19

A) 2str: "no way to be sure of preventing blackouts" is the danger phrase. It's too extreme of a statement.

B) NM: "academic or personal success" are the danger phrase. It's not mentioned.

C) 2sp: "people with a family history" is the danger word. The recommendation includes a larger group.

d) **ANSWER: family history = "a large number of alcoholic relatives (line 93) control their consumption = "drink moderately (line 89-90).**

20

A) NM: memory impairment "occurs" during a blackout is the danger word. Does not talk about the method of preventing blackouts.

B) NM: the lines talk about a phenomenon of alcoholic blackouts "resolved spontaneously (danger word)," not a method to prevent it.

C) NM: a statement of people who are "genetically more vulnerable(danger word)" to blackouts, not a method for prevention.

D) **ANSWER: suggests a clear set of recommendations to prevent blackouts.**

Passage 3

21

A) NM: limitations of existing studies were mentioned (line 19-22), but the paragraph talks about recent studies and a hypothesis that already addressed these limitations. So "proposes" and "specific methods" are danger words.

B) NM: the second paragraph "identified factors," but the terms were already clear. So "clarifying confusing terms" is the danger phrase.

C) **ANSWER: presents a hypothesis = (line 24-26)**

D) NM: "new way of thinking" is the danger word. The field is already familiar with factors such as sex and status.

22

A) 2str: "intense" refers to "a lot of" here, but doesn't mean it's too much.

B) 2str: "fierce" is another synonym of intense, but it refers to a vigorous manner, which is too extreme for the context.

C) **ANSWER: refers to the amount of interest generated. Suits the tone.**

d) 2str: interest cannot be sharp.

23

A) **ANSWER: managing social relationships = "when too many females are present for the alpha to guard (line 34-35) share rewards with a lower status male = "sharing matings occurs between the alpha male and the second ranked male (line 36-67)."**

B) NM: "food supply" is the danger word, not

mentioned.

C) NM: "genetic diversity" is the danger word, not mentioned.

D) NM: instead of "limiting group size," males share matings.

24

A) 2gen: lines talk about "several factors," instead of explaining why a male shares a reward.

B) NI: the hypothesis states males "share rewards," but not why.

C) **ANSWER: lines talk about a situation in which sharing a reward occurs and why.**

D) NI: talks about between whom sharing a reward occurs, not why.

25

A) **ANSWER: men are more likely than women to share rewards with same-sex colleagues of lower status = "human males are more likely than high status females to cooperate with lower status same-sex individuals. (line 65-68)"**

B) OPP: "no differences" is the danger word, there IS a difference.

C) OPP: "both" are the danger word, men share rewards with a lower status males more frequently.

D) NM: "prefer" is the danger word, which is not mentioned in the passage.

26

A) 2gen: does not detail the difference.

B) **ANSWER: explains that males are more likely to share rewards with a lower-status males than females are.**

C) NI: same-sex individuals interacting with "identical high status" is the danger word. This is only partially mentioned in c and d in question 25.

D) NM: men "perceiving" (danger word) lower-status males "more positively" (danger word) are not mentioned in any answer choices in question 25.

27

A) NM: synonym of "invest in" in terms of economics, which does not fit the context.

B) 2str: "invest in" means to help here, which does not automatically "establish" them in an important position.

C) NM: bankroll means supply of money, which does not fit the context.

D) **ANSWER: "invest in" here means to support, which nearly means.**

28

A) NM: "increasing the bonding" of "males" is not directly related to women being hindered in their professional success.

B) NM: "different types of investment" is the danger word. Does not talk about hindering professional success.

C) NM: suggests a solution to women not investing in their lower-ranked peers. "encourage" is the danger word.

D) **ANSWER: "struggles of women in the workplace" suggests workplace dynamics hindering their professional success. making** "career ladder more equitable for women" suggests that currently women do not enjoy as much professional success as men do.

29

A) Not correct. High influence males column is smaller than low influence males column.

B) **ANSWER: Both columns of lower influence participants are the highest.**

C) NM: not clear from the graph. 'Partner' can be low influence or high influence male or female.

D) Not correct. Low influence males are more likely.

30

A) OPP: "Directly refutes" is the danger word. Although the exact numbers are different, proportion of each group in Figure 2 is similar to Figure 1.

B) OPP: both figures are about human men and women.

C) **ANSWER: Figure 2 mentions "mean number of dollars shared," which is more specific than "proportion shared" in Figure 1. Also, Figure 2 supports Figure 1.**

D) OPP: "strongly undermine" is the danger word because Figure 2 supports Figure 1.

Passage 4

31

A) Y: when tree "bears" a fruit, it produces a fruit.

B) NM: uphold means to support, which is out of context.

C) NM: synonym of "bears," but out of context.

D) OPP: tree does not take a fruit.

32

A) NM: the passage does not talk about producing "useful citizens", so this is the danger phrase.

B) NM: "ultimately useful tool" again is the danger word.

C) OPP: "only by recognizing that what is natural is good" is the danger phrase. According to the author, society and nature cannot coexist.

D) **ANSWER: artificial construct = "the public institute... cannot exist ... there is neither country nor patriot (line 32)" serves no useful purpose = "the very words should be struck out of our language (line 33-34)"**

33

A) NM: talks about human tendency to destroy things nature made, not society.

B) NM: talks about human tendency to avoid sensations, not society.

C) **ANSWER: society is mentioned as the public institute, which is then described as artificial construct.**

D) NM: talks about inner conflicts, not society.

34

A) OPP: "wholly perfect" is the danger phrase. Natural impulses are sometimes not desirable. (line 54)

B) 2str: "guidelines" is the danger word. It should be taken account of, but to make them into guidelines is too extreme.

C) OPP: "irrelevant" is the danger word because there are some desirable natural impulses (line 58)

D) **ANSWER: not necessarily good = "does not follow that these tendencies are all desirable (line 54-55) but also must not be ignored in education = "but it does follow that since they are there, they are operative and must be taken account of (line 55-57).**

35

A) **ANSWER: educational reformers claim that education is important, which means they advocate importance of education.**

B) 2str: plead is to beg, which is too extreme in the context.

C) 2str: reformers claim it's important, but they do not force the importance upon others.

D) NM: urge can be used as a noun to mean desire, but not in this context.

36

A) NM: "long periods" is the danger word. Time is not mentioned in regards to dissatisfaction with society. (but with education)

B) NM: "inequalities" is the danger word, not the topic of the passage.

C) **ANSWER: dissatisfaction with society = "that artificiality against which the conception of following nature is largely a protest (line 65-67)" children being compelled by adults to conform with adult values = "attempts to force children directly into the mold of grown-up standards. (line 67)."**

D) NM: "beauty of nature" is the danger word. The author is not talking about literal nature, but human nature.

37

A) NM: talks about natural tendencies to be manifested in children, not dissatisfaction with society.

B) **ANSWER: Showing natural tendencies is a protest = dissatisfaction with society. It results from children being forced to conform to adult standards.**

C) NM: talks about the development of idea of following nature, not dissatisfaction with society.

D) NM: talks about idea of mind being used to pretend there are no differences among people.

38

A) 2str: "logical absurdity" is the danger word. The author of one partially agrees with the author of Passage 1. "has its significance (line 101-102)" "that...is true enough (line 111)"

B) NM: "policy" is the danger word. It was not mentioned.

C) **ANSWER: The author suggests what to do at the end of the passage: "not to educate apart...**

but rather to provide an environment in which native powers will be put to better uses (line 111-114)" after conceding the author 1's point about evils of society.

D) OPP: "reaffirm" is the danger word. The author 2 suggests a different conclusion.

39

A) ANSWER: Passage 2 elaborates upon the idea of natural tendencies and education and adds different nuances on conclusions of Passage 1.

B) NM: "benefits" and "proposals" are the danger words. Passage 1 does not propose anything but concludes with a dismal view of the situation.

C) 2str: Passage 2 does find Passage 1 convincing to some degree, so "fail to find redeeming value" is the danger phrase that is too strong.

D) NM: Passage 2 does not propose "programs (danger word)".

40

A) 2str: "completely" is the danger word. Passage 2 talks about balancing between society and nature.

B) NM: "can" is the danger word. Passage 1 thinks public education cannot make room for what is natural.

C) ANSWER: both passages talk about how individual natures are often in conflict with social norms.

D) NM: both passage argue that individuals have different abilities, not "equal abilities (danger word).

41

A) OPP: Passage 1 thinks human beings have to choose between nature and society, so mixing the two is not idealistic.

B) ANSWER: Passage 1 says "we make a compromise and reach neither goal." also, "we...die before we have found peace."

C) OPP: To passage 1, reconciling society and nature are not "necessary," it is impossible.

D) 2str: Passage 1 simply says it is not possible.

Passage 5

42

A) OPP: "undermine" and "neutrality" are danger words. It is clear throughout the passage that the author is optimistic about renewable energy.

B) OPP: "mixed emotion" and "reservations" are danger words. The words in fifth paragraph is hopeful and there is opposite to reservations.

C) OPP: "ironic" is incorrect because the author genuinely believes that the technology is novel. He describes this in detail.

D) ANSWER: By using words that are positive, the author is showing the possibility of bias towards the technology. These adjectives and adverbs are subjective.

43

A) ANSWER: provide energy generation in a diverse number of situations = "a plethora of opportunities exist (line 99)"

B) 2str: "primary" is the danger word. The passage cannot predict this.

C) 2str: "too expensive" is the danger word. Although "the cost" is briefly mentioned, it is to point out that PV is cheaper than silicon based PV energy.

D) OPP: "neither" generate "enough electricity" when "forced to interact" is not true. HPP (combination of PV and piezoelectric) can "provide almost uninterrupted energy generation (line 80-81)".

44

A) 2gen: the lines state that PV energy is one of the most significant alternative energy harvesters, but does not explain why this is so.

B) NI: The lines merely state various ways in which energy can be generated, not situations where energy generation is provided.

C) NI: It's describing the historical background of energy generation, not the technology in question.

D) ANSWER: describes why it's promising in regards to energy generation.

45

A) 2str: "too inflexible" is the danger word. It has been made flexible. (Line 74-75)

B) OPP: "will eventually" are danger words. Sun energy already does that.

C) ANSWER: the percentage of converted energy has increased from 1-2% to 24.7%. It has increased in efficiency dramatically. (line 27-31)

D) 2str: "will eventually" is the danger phrase. The passage merely says efficiency of PV energy is "important" to make it competitive with fossil fuels. (line 25-27)

46

*** line reference needs to be fixed ***

A) NM: talks about sun energy, not about PV technology development.

B) NI: compares PV energy to fossil fuels. Not related to answer C.

C) ANSWER: describes that technology has increased in efficiency (=development).

D) NM: limited applications are not mentioned in answer C.

47

A) OPP: impulse implies the notion is a desire or is spontaneous. Neither definition fits the context.

B) NM: the notion is a whole idea, not a clue.

C) NM: the notion here means a statement, not an image.

D) ANSWER: a notion here is Coulomb's theory, a synonym of proposition.

48

A) ANSWER: possible uses = "small electronic devices, tree structure, textile structures…"

B) 2sp: "aesthetic benefits" is the danger phrase. It is only one of many advantages of HPP detailed in the paragraph.

C) OPP: "dangers" is the danger word. The paragraph talks about potential benefits of HPP.

D) 2str: "majority" is the danger word. Talks about potential benefits, but does not go far as to state it will provide the majority of human electrical demand.

49

A) OPP: the passage is dedicated to detailing how using HPP is near future.

B) 2sp: "intriguing" and "engineers" are danger words. The passage does not talk about engineers' interests. The trace amount of electricity captured has merely increased. (line 7-8)

C) OPP: "unreliable" is the danger word. Flexibility of HPP has made it reliable.

D) ANSWER: Engineers are looking for ways to replace fossil fuels. (line 25-27)

50

A) this is efficiency, not resistance rate.

B) efficiency is medium for BaTiO3.

C) ANSWER: PZT= greatest efficiency. Resistance = 1,200.

D) efficiency is the lowest.

51

a) medium density. Lowest voltage.

B) highest density. Medium voltage.

C) ANSWER: lowest density = PVDF highest voltage = PVDF

d) not true.

52

A) NM: "insufficient data points" is the danger word. The graph provides NO information on weight.

B) ANSWER: The graph only provides the various factors. No link can be established.

C) NM: density is not weight. We need mass.

D) NM: No information on weight.

Part 1

SAT® Practice Test #4

Reading Test

65 MINUTES, 52 QUESTIONS

Turn to Section 1 of your answer sheet to answer the questions in this section.

DIRECTIONS

Each passage or pair of passages below is followed by a number of questions. After reading each passage or pair, choose the best answer to each question based on what is stated or implied in the passage or passages and in any accompanying graphics (such as a table or graph).

Questions 1-11 are based on the following passage.

This passage is adapted from *Don Quixote* by Miguel De Cervantes. Originally published in 1615.

Don Quixote called the landlord of the inn, and shutting himself into the stable with him, fell on his knees before him, saying, "From this spot I rise not, valiant knight, until your courtesy grants me the boon
5 I seek, one that will redound to your praise and the benefit of the human race." The landlord, seeing his guest at his feet and hearing a speech of this kind, stood staring at him in bewilderment, not knowing what to do or say, and entreating him to rise, but all
10 to no purpose until he had agreed to grant the boon demanded of him. "I looked for no less, my lord, from your High Magnificence," replied Don Quixote, "and I have to tell you that the boon I have asked and your liberality has granted is that you shall dub
15 me knight to-morrow morning, and that to-night I shall watch my arms in the chapel of this your castle; thus tomorrow, as I have said, will be accomplished what I so much desire, enabling me lawfully to roam through all the four quarters of the world seeking
20 adventures on behalf of those in distress, as is the duty of chivalry and of knights-errant like myself, whose ambition is directed to such deeds."

The landlord, who, as has been mentioned, was something of a wag, and had already some suspicion
25 of his guest's want of wits, was quite convinced of it on hearing talk of this kind from him, and to make sport for the night he determined to fall in with his humour. So he told him he was quite right in pursuing the object he had in view, and that such a
30 motive was natural and becoming in cavaliers as distinguished as he seemed and his gallant bearing showed him to be; and that he himself in his younger days had followed the same honourable calling, roaming in quest of adventures in various
35 parts of the world, where he had proved the nimbleness of his feet and the lightness of his fingers, doing many wrongs, cheating many widows, ruining maids and swindling minors, and, in short, bringing himself under the notice of almost every
40 tribunal and court of justice in Spain; until at last he had retired to this castle of his, where he was living upon his property and upon that of others; and where he received all knights-errant of whatever rank or condition they might be, all for the great love he
45 bore them and that they might share their substance with him in return for his benevolence.

Don Quixote promised to follow his advice scrupulously, and it was arranged forthwith that he should watch his armour in a large yard at one side
50 of the inn; so, collecting it all together, Don Quixote placed it on a trough that stood by the side of a well, and bracing his buckler on his arm he grasped his lance and began with a stately air to march up and down in front of the trough, and as he began
55 his march night began to fall.

The landlord told all the people who were in the inn about the craze of his guest, the watching of the armour, and the dubbing ceremony he contemplated. Full of wonder at so strange a form of madness, they flocked to see it from a distance, and observed with what composure he sometimes paced up and down, or sometimes, leaning on his lance, gazed on his armour without taking his eyes off it for ever so long; and as the night closed in with a light from the moon so brilliant that it might vie with his that lent it, everything the novice knight did was plainly seen by all.

Meanwhile one of the carriers who were in the inn thought fit to water his team, and it was necessary to remove Don Quixote's armour as it lay on the trough; but he seeing the other approach hailed him in a loud voice, "O thou, whoever thou art, rash knight that comest to lay hands on the armour of the most valorous errant that ever girt on sword, have a care what thou dost; touch it not unless thou wouldst lay down thy life as the penalty of thy rashness." The carrier gave no heed to these words (and he would have done better to heed them if he had been heedful of his health), but seizing it by the straps flung the armour some distance from him. Seeing this, Don Quixote raised his eyes to heaven, and fixing his thoughts, apparently, upon his lady Dulcinea, exclaimed, "Aid me, lady mine, in this the first encounter that presents itself to this breast which thou holdest in subjection; let not thy favour and protection fail me in this first jeopardy;" and, with these words and others to the same purpose, dropping his buckler he lifted his lance with both hands and with it smote such a blow on the carrier's head that he stretched him on the ground, so stunned that had he followed it up with a second there would have been no need of a surgeon to cure him. This done, he picked up his armour and returned to his beat with the same serenity as before.

1

Which choice best summarizes the passage?
A) A humorous story is invented to impress a noble lady.
B) A deeply confused man is humored by a businessman, leading to disastrous consequences.
C) A knight is honored by a lord, but the ceremony ends in disaster.
D) During the performance of a comedic play, two men quarrel over a woman.

2

As used in line 13, "boon" most nearly means
A) detriment.
B) compensation.
C) benefaction.
D) prosperity.

3

As used in line 35, "proved" most nearly means
A) considered.
B) evaluated.
C) hardened.
D) demonstrated.

4

According to the passage, why does the landlord pretend to believe Don Quixote?
A) He wishes to spend an entertaining night by humoring Don Quixote.
B) He has his own adventurous stories that he wants to share with Don Quixote.
C) He realizes that Don Quixote's psychological state might put him in danger.
D) He hopes to assist Don Quixote in overcoming his delusions.

5

Which of the following choices provides the best evidence for the answer to the previous question?
A) Lines 23-28 ("The landlord...humour")
B) Lines 28-32 ("So he...be")
C) Lines 32-38 ("and that...minors")
D) Lines 42-46 ("and where...benevolence")

6

The passage strongly suggests that Don Quixote decides to guard his armour because
A) he believes the landlord's lies are real.
B) he hopes to avoid paying for his room.
C) he wants to avoid offending the landlord.
D) he does not want to anger the lady Dulcinea.

7

The description in lines 59-64 ("Full...long") mainly serves to
A) emphasize the extent of Don Quixote's eccentric behavior.
B) illustrate the size of the village population.
C) establish Don Quixote's skill in both performance and combat.
D) contrast the crowd's horror to Don Quixote's calm.

8

Based on the passage, what does "this first jeopardy" in line 86 refer to?
A) Don Quixote's unwavering love for lady Dulcinea
B) Don Quixote's impending battle with the carrier
C) Don Quixote's initial encounter with lady Dulcinea
D) Don Quixote's most important consideration as a knight

9

As used in line 90, "stunned" most nearly means
A) amazed.
B) speechless.
C) disoriented.
D) startled.

10

According to the passage, which of the following best explains why Don Quixote strikes the carrier?
A) The carrier touched his armour.
B) The carrier belittled him.
C) The carrier insulted lady Dulcinea.
D) The carrier tried to steal his sword.

11

Which of the following choices provides the best evidence for the answer to the previous question?
A) Lines 68-71 ("Meanwhile...trough")
B) Lines 75-81 ("touch...him")
C) Lines 81-85 ("Don Quixote...subjection")
D) Lines 88-92 ("he lifted...him")

Questions 12-22 are based on the following passage and supplementary materials.

This passage is adapted from "The nexus of oil, conflict, and climate change vulnerability of pastoral communities in northwest Kenya" by J. Schilling, R. Locham, et. al., 2015.

According to the UN World Factbook, agriculture and pastoralism are the dominant sources for food production and income generation in Africa. Especially
Line in arid and semi-arid regions such as Turkana in
5 northwest Kenya, pastoralism is a well-suited livelihood and production system that makes efficient use of the highly limited water and pasture resources. But pastoralism across the African continent is often viewed by national governments as being "backward"
10 and partly even "primitive." Views like these have resulted in political, economic and social marginalization and discrimination of pastoral communities. Turkana is no exception. Here, the limitation of pastoral mobility by the government of
15 Kenya and neighboring governments has decreased the adaptive capability of pastoralists.

In this conflict-ridden area, significant oil reserves have recently been discovered. The dimensions are immense. The main basin in Turkana alone contains
20 more than 600 million barrels of oil according to the UK-based operating company Tullow Oil. The commercial viability has been confirmed and Tullow's exploration director concludes that "northern Kenya has the potential to become a significant new hydrocarbon
25 province." For the government of Kenya the discovery of oil is very good news. For the pastoral communities the effects of the oil exploration are likely to be more ambivalent. But how ambivalent? A review of existing studies on pastoralism and oil
30 provides little to answer this question, because there are very few studies on oil exploration, pastoralism, and conflict. For Kenya there has only been one study; the authors concluded that oil is part of "a tinderbox of risk for violent conflict, lawlessness, and
35 potential armed rebellion."

Most other studies on the topic have focused on (South) Sudan. For pastoralists in Sudan already confronted with militarization of inter-ethnic conflicts and displacement, oil is an additional worry. These
40 have concluded that "oil has not engendered peace and prosperity but the exact opposite." Further, unmet expectations of pastoralists for employment in the oil sector have led to attacks on oil sites and contributed to insecurity.

45 But these studies also find positive aspects in oil exploitation. The road infrastructure and hence mobility has improved as a result of the presence of the oil industry. Along the oil roads new settlements and markets have emerged, opening new opportunities
50 for trade and development. Beyond (South) Sudan, there are several studies exploring the effects of oil exploitation on communities. Particularly in Nigeria, the detrimental effects of oil exploitation on the communities are well studied. Given the significant
55 revenues earned with oil and the persistent high levels of insecurity and urban poverty, oil has mostly become a "resource curse" for communities in rural Nigeria. For example, unfair distribution of oil revenues has been reported as a major cause of
60 attacks on oil pipelines and raids of oil sites.

In conjunction with the ongoing process of devolution, the government of Kenya needs to ensure a fair and transparent sharing of oil revenues between the different levels of government and especially the
65 local communities. The county government needs to use the financial assets received through devolution and the oil revenues to make up for its failure in Turkana. This means making significant investments into education, health services, and water and
70 transport infrastructure. In particular, the development of the significant aquifers found in Turkana needs to be prioritized to improve the water availability for the communities. The oil pipelines, roads and railways need to be built without disrupting existing pastoral
75 migration routes and grazing land. The issue of land rights has to be addressed to prevent the communities from losing their land without proper compensation. The local government needs to offer communication channels for local communities to allow them to
80 express their concerns and requests directly.

Finally, the issue of insecurity and violent conflict needs to be addressed through intercommunal peace meetings, especially between the Turkana. Community liaison officers (CLOs) are a promising approach.
85 They allow Tullow and any oil company operating in Turkana to closely communicate with the local communities to inform them about the operations, get their feedback and, manage their expectations. Although demand for unskilled labor in the oil

industry is limited, integration of Turkana into the
company's workforce will be a positive sign for the
communities. To be able to increase the share of
Turkana employees, it is important to offer training
possibilities in which community members can acquire
skills needed in the oil industry. If every actor,
particularly the government of Kenya and Tullow,
takes these recommendations seriously, then there is a
real chance that Turkana and Kenya overall can
benefit from the oil. Unfortunately, the more likely
scenario is that oil will exacerbate the existing
marginalization and discrimination of pastoral
communities, which in turn is likely to fuel more
conflict.

12

Over the course of the passage, the main focus shifts from
A) a description of current conflicts in a geographic area and its devastating effects on the companies involved in its development.
B) an overview of the social and economic conflicts in an area to an examination of potential solutions to those problems.
C) a discussion of the history of the global oil industry in Africa to assessment of its damage to local communities.
D) a historical overview of the development of pastoralism to its relationship with the oil industry

13

As used in line 22, "viability" most nearly means
A) possibility.
B) liveliness.
C) energy.
D) impulse.

14

It can be reasonably inferred from the passage that the author thinks pastoralism in Africa
A) is "backwards" because of Africa's limited water sources.
B) is limited in its ability to expand beyond the African continent.
C) is enhanced by the advent of oil industry in Africa.
D) is negatively affected by government policies.

15

Which choice provides the best evidence for the answer to the previous question?
A) Lines 7-10 ("But...primitive")
B) Lines 13-16 ("Here...pastoralists")
C) Lines 26-28 ("For...ambivalent")
D) Lines 37-39 ("For...worry")

16

Which choice provides the best evidence for the claim that oil exploitation brings about positive effects?
A) Lines 46-48 ("The road...industry")
B) Lines 52-54 ("Particularly...studied")
C) Lines 58-60 ("For...sites")
D) Lines 65-68 ("The...Turkana")

17

The rhetorical question "But how ambivalent?" in line 28 best serves to
A) indicate the significance of recent studies on the relationship between pastoralism and oil industry.
B) reassert claims made by the author earlier in the passage.
C) show that a lack of studies prevents scholars from reaching a definite conclusion.
D) express concerns about awareness of the potential negative effects of the oil exploration.

18

As used in line 40, "engendered" most nearly means
A) promoted.
B) evolved.
C) inflamed.
D) incited.

19

The author's comment about community liaison officers (CLOs) is most likely intended to
A) encourage the communication between the oil companies.
B) highlight the promising future of the African pastoralism.
C) provide an example of a potential solution to existing conflicts.
D) praise the Turkana communities for effective communication.

20

The passage implies that the author's attitude towards oil industry operations in Africa is
A) critical.
B) optimistic.
C) neutral.
D) disinterested.

21

Which choice provides the best evidence for the answer to the previous question?
A) Lines 81-83 ("Finally...Turkana")
B) Lines 85-89 ("They...expectations")
C) Lines 92-95 ("To...industry")
D) Lines 99-103 ("Unfortunately...conflict")

22

It can be reasonably be inferred from the passage that even though the demand for unskilled labor in oil industry is low, oil companies will be helpful if
A) revenues are divided between oil companies and the government.
B) the indigenous population is employed.
C) the government can regulate the workforce.
D) they invest heavily in the promotion of pastoralism.

Questions 23-32 are based on the following passages.

Passage 1 is adapted from "Problematic Smartphone Use, Deep and Surface Approaches to Learning, and Social Media Use in Lectures" by Dmitri Rozgonjuk, Kristiina Saal and Karin Taht, 2018. Passage 2 is adapted from "Language in the Wild—Living in the Carnival in Social Media" by Sylvi Vigmo and Annika Lantz-Andersson, 2014.

Passage 1

Since their introduction in 2009, smartphones have had a significant impact on daily life across the world. The worldwide ownership of smartphones is around 43%. Smartphones have several advantages in educational settings, allowing one to take notes, browse for information, communicate with others, and use specific applications for learning skills. Several studies have shown, however, that there are instances where the excessive use of smartphones leads to the development of "problematic smartphone use" (PSU), a phenomenon characterized by the occurrence of addictive-like symptoms. Imagine, for example, a student who spends more time managing their appearance on their various social media accounts than they do interacting with their peers and meeting their academic responsibilities. PSU has been associated with psychopathological symptoms as well as poor academic outcomes. Similar findings have been reported with excessive social media use. What is yet unknown is how PSU relates to learning. Specifically, how PSU might interfere with student understanding (known as the deep approach to learning) and learning motivated by external incentives (for example, grades; known as a surface approach to learning). By contrast, some studies have shown improved student retention of information from lectures due to social media interaction specifically about the contents of the lecture.

Previous studies regarding smartphone addiction are often seen as controversial. It has been debated whether or not smartphone "addiction" is a behavioral addiction, and whether or not it may be considered as an actual addiction from the perspective of contemporary addiction theories. Nevertheless, one cannot neglect the growing body of evidence that suggests that problematic smartphone usage is related to several psychopathological symptoms, such as depression and anxiety, poorer health and sleep quality, and lower academic achievements. In essence, the excessive use of smartphones is accompanied by symptoms resembling those found in contemporary addiction models: dependence, withdrawal, tolerance, and functional impairment; therefore, we conceptualize the phenomenon as problematic smartphone use.

Passage 2

After decades of research on the roles of information technology and its relations to the learning sciences, there are expectations that comprise exaggerated promises of how information technology will revolutionize schooling and transform the very nature of learning. However, such assumptions have also been criticized for being seductive and biased. In retrospect, new technologies have been investigated with high expectations of positive development for organized education, which is in need of pedagogical change.

Examining the relationship between education and social media and smartphone activity is a promising avenue of research. Some of the most important traits of a healthy education involve participation and engagement, characteristics that social media and smartphone usage encourages. Today's social media has proliferated at a remarkable speed through the Internet. Social media as part of everyday life has been explored as sites in which young people, among other activities, engage in identity work, that is, performing online the way they want others to look at them. Understanding how young people shape their identities can lead to changes in educational strategies. As a research area, this has led to increasing numbers of studies investigating what these changed conditions for engagement afford, and what constraints can be discussed when social media is moving away from its original self-directed practices, to practices based on institutional education.

Social media sites and smartphones have been examined as spaces for the ongoing development of young people's individual or collective identities, which are continuously negotiated for the public view. One specific concern in social media, is that the conditions for engaging have changed not only the context but also the connection to an audience, whether real, assumed or both. What has been conceptualized previously as social performance, although mostly in relation to earlier media such as TV, can still be useful to apply. Activities such as updating your status and profile can be seen as part of your social performance, how you want others to see you, in other words how you frame the situation

as a kind of performance. Research displays similar
90results regarding the development of social identity as
closely interlinked with intentions of how you present
yourself online, as part of management impression.
Working on your profile and updating your status is
argued to be a kind of performance, and that by
95experimenting with images, you are writing yourself
into being. Furthermore, understanding the
performance aspect of social media is important, since
young people are often thought to perform and
present themselves in different ways in classroom
100settings.

23

Which statement best describes the relationship between the two passages?
A) Passage 1 argues against the authenticity of the evidence presented in Passage 2.
B) Passage 1 takes a different approach to a phenomenon analyzed in Passage 2.
C) Passage 1 expands on an educational theory discussed in Passage 2.
D) Passage 1 elaborates on a study cited in Passage 2.

24

Which statement summarizes an important difference between the two passages?
A) Passage 1 describes the potential disadvantages of using a smartphone, while Passage 2 focuses on its social impact on young people.
B) Passage 1 lists several arguments against using a smartphone, while Passage 2 debunks misconceptions regarding smartphone addiction.
C) Passage 1 cites a recent study to discuss educational benefits of smartphone usage, while Passage 2 relies on conventional theories regarding smartphone usage.
D) Passage 1 offers a general overview of smartphone usage, while Passage 2 discusses the psychological impact that smartphone usage has on young people.

25

In line 49, "revolutionize" most nearly means
A) revamp.
B) outshine.
C) democratize.
D) overshadow.

26

The author of Passage 1 considers "the excessive use of smartphones" (line 9) to be
A) educational.
B) negligible.
C) lamentable.
D) temporary.

27

The statement in lines 34-39 ("Nevertheless...achievements") is best described as
A) a persuasive statement.
B) a definite rejection.
C) a reluctant concession.
D) an emotional plea.

28

The "changed conditions" (line 70) are best described as
A) the differing identities of social media users.
B) the personal expression allowed by social media usage.
C) detrimental effects brought about by social media.
D) the increasing bias of social media users.

29

Which choice provides the best evidence for the answer to the previous question?
A) Lines 45-50 ("After decades...learning")
B) Lines 50-51 ("However...biased")
C) Lines 61-63 ("Today's...Internet")
D) Lines 63-67 ("Social...them")

30

The statement in lines 82-85 ("What...apply") primarily serves to
A) admit a counterargument regarding performance.
B) create a connection between concepts.
C) refute an outdated notion.
D) prove the usefulness of a theory.

31

Which choice provides the best evidence for the claim that social media helps young people establish their identities?
A) Lines 4-7 ("Smartphones...skills")
B) Lines 24-28 ("By contrast...lecture")
C) Lines 52-55 ("In retrospect...change")
D) Lines 89-92 ("Research...impression")

32

The author of Passage 1 would likely characterize the "working on your profile" (line 93) as
A) alarming because it is one of the known causes of social media addiction.
B) dangerous because it exposes the user's identity to the general public.
C) interesting because it allows expansion of relationships.
D) concerning because it may be an example of problematic smartphone use.

Questions 33-42 are based on the following passage.

This passage is adapted from *Washington's Farewell Address*, a speech given by George Washington in 1796.

　　For encouraging a common bond, you have every inducement of sympathy and interest. Citizens, by birth or choice, of a common country, that country has a right to concentrate your affections. The name
5 of American, which belongs to you in your national capacity, must always exalt the just pride of patriotism more than any appellation derived from local discriminations. With slight shades of difference, you have the same religion, manners, habits, and
10 political principles. You have in a common cause fought and triumphed together; the independence and liberty you possess are the work of joint counsels, and joint efforts of common dangers, sufferings, and successes.
15　　But these considerations, however powerfully they address themselves to your sensibility, are greatly outweighed by those which apply more immediately to your interest. Here every portion of our country finds the most commanding motives for carefully
20 guarding and preserving the union of the whole.
　　The North, in an unrestrained intercourse with the South, protected by the equal laws of a common government, finds in the productions of the latter great additional resources of maritime and commercial
25 enterprise and precious materials of manufacturing industry. The South, in the same intercourse, sees its agriculture grow and its commerce expand. Turning partly into its own channels the seamen of the North, it finds its particular navigation invigorated; and it
30 looks forward to the protection of a maritime strength. The East, in a like intercourse with the West, already finds, and will continue to find a valuable vent for the commodities which it brings from abroad, or manufactures at home. The West
35 derives from the East supplies requisite to its growth and comfort, and, what is perhaps of still greater consequence, it must of necessity owe the secure enjoyment of indispensable outlets for its own productions to the weight, influence, and the future
40 maritime strength of the Atlantic side of the Union, directed by an indissoluble community of interest as one nation.

　　While, then, every part of our country thus feels an immediate and particular interest in union, all the
45 parts combined cannot fail to find in the united mass of means and efforts greater strength, greater resource, proportionably greater security from external danger, a less frequent interruption of their peace by foreign nations; and, what is of inestimable
50 value, they must derive from union an exemption from those broils and wars between themselves, which their local rivalries alone would be sufficient to produce, but which opposite foreign alliances, attachments, and intrigues would stimulate and
55 embitter even more. Hence, likewise, they will avoid the necessity of those overgrown military establishments which, under any form of government, are inauspicious to liberty, and which are to be regarded as particularly hostile to republican liberty.
60 In this sense it is that your union ought to be considered as a main prop of your liberty, and that the love of the one ought to endear to you the preservation of the other.
　　These considerations speak a persuasive language
65 to every reflecting and virtuous mind, and exhibit the continuance of the Union as a primary object of patriotic desire. Is there a doubt whether a common government can embrace so large a sphere? Let experience solve it. To listen to mere speculation in
70 such a case were criminal. We are authorized to hope that a proper organization of the whole with the auxiliary agency of governments for the respective subdivisions, will afford a happy issue to the experiment. It is well worth a fair and full
75 experiment. With such powerful and obvious motives to union, affecting all parts of our country, while experience shall not have demonstrated its impracticability, there will always be reason to distrust the patriotism of those who in any quarter
80 may endeavor to weaken its bands.

33

The author's central claim in the passage is that
A) a country should try multiple types of governments.
B) the government should focus on overcoming enemies.
C) all parts of the country should strive for unity.
D) the North and the South should engage in international trade.

34

The main difference Washington draws between the South and the North is that
A) the South specializes in agriculture, while the North is known for its manufacturing and trade.
B) the South develops transportation over land, while the North does so by sea.
C) the South is against international trade, while the North supports international connections.
D) the South develops its industry, while the North develops its agriculture.

35

As used in line 4, "to concentrate" most nearly means
A) to condense.
B) to draw.
C) to summarize.
D) to purify.

36

The author mentions that national unity promotes
A) the expansion of territory.
B) economic activity.
C) strong governmental control.
D) an exchange of cultures.

37

Which choice provides the best evidence for the answer to the previous question?
A) Lines 1-4 ("For...affections")
B) Lines 10-14 ("You...successes")
C) Lines 18-20 ("Here...whole")
D) Lines 31-34 ("The East...home")

38

In the passage, Washington repeats the word "greater" in lines 46-47 in order to
A) allude to the past expansion of the regions involved.
B) emphasize the vast difference that exists between different nations.
C) warn against the possible civil war that might arise.
D) emphasize the benefits that will arise from a unified country.

39

As used in line 59, "hostile" most nearly means
A) permanent.
B) adverse.
C) bitter.
D) indifferent.

40

In the fourth paragraph (lines 43-63), Washington identifies which of the following as a direct threat to freedom?
A) A government that expands its territory by colonizing other countries.
B) A government that neglects its allies abroad.
C) A government that is involved in unnecessary foreign affairs.
D) A government that fails to upkeep its military establishment.

41

What does Washington imply by "Let experience solve it" in lines 68-69?
A) The motivations for unity are greater than the potential risks.
B) Experiences will reveal weaknesses of a unified government.
C) The current outrage over a common government will disappear over time
D) Opportunities like these rarely present themselves in history.

42

Which choice best represents Washington's opinion of a citizen's duty?
A) Lines 37-40 ("it ... Union")
B) Lines 49-51 ("what ... themselves")
C) Lines 64-67 ("These ... desire")
D) Lines 70-75 ("We ... experiment")

Questions 43-52 are based on the following passage and supplementary material.

This passage is adapted from "Differences in play can illuminate differences in affiliation: A comparative study on chimpanzees and gorillas" by Giada Cordoni, Ivan Norscia, Maria Bobbio and Elisabetta Palagi, 2018.

Compared to 'serious' behaviors, whose functions are immediately evident (e.g., sexual behavior, aggressive behavior), play is a difficult behavior to contextualize from both a functional and an operational point of view. When we talk about play we immediately think about its long-term benefits, such as cognitive and social skill improvement. However, play also has short-term benefits that are not always obvious to the observer. It has been demonstrated that play can reduce social anxiety linked to particular contexts such as crowded condition, pre-feeding competition, and sexual competition.

Recent findings on the distribution of play as a function of sex, age, relationship quality, and distribution of power, suggest that play can be shaped according to the social structure and the inter-individual relationships that characterize each group. If play is fair and cooperative, it can serve to establish social relationships; on the contrary, if play is highly unbalanced and competitive, it will be used to improve ranking status. The short-term adaptive functions of play can be related to the level of cooperation and tolerance of the species considered. For example, adult play rates generally co-vary with the level of tolerance and social affiliation characterizing the group. Inter-individual tolerance favors the retention of play also during the adult phase, thus suggesting that this behavior can provide benefits also during adulthood. In particular, play between adults and unrelated juveniles can be used as a "social bridge" strategy to expand the social network of adults. Indeed, play has proved a reliable tool to strengthen social bonding, especially in those species (such as chimpanzees) that are highly cohesive and cooperative.

Despite their genetic closeness, chimpanzees and lowland gorillas differ in their social organization. Chimpanzees live in the so-called fission-fusion society formed by several reproductive males and adult females with their offspring. Males are mostly kin-related and, consistently, highly sociable and cooperative; they cement their relationships via grooming, sharing food and supporting each-other during aggressive encounters as well as in territorial defense. In some wild communities and in captivity, a certain level of sociality can be also found between females who engage in grooming sessions and agonistic support and establish long-term relationships. In general, grooming is frequent in both wild and captive chimpanzees, which can use it as a social investment strategy also to gain reproductive advantages.

The western lowland gorilla, another primate species, lives in breeding groups that usually comprise one adult male (silverback), several adult females and immature offspring. In the wild, female gorillas must associate with a silverback male primarily to avoid infanticide. Yet, vulnerability to large terrestrial predators, such as leopards, can also lead to male-female spatial association. Following the death of a leading male, groups typically disintegrate and females seek the protection of a new silverback male by joining new groups. Adult females rarely interact in active ways. Indeed, helpful interactions, such as grooming, are rare. For example, in a study on a wild population of lowland gorillas, grooming was never observed except for mothers who occasionally groomed infants less than 2 years old.

The distribution of helpful and protective support in the chimpanzee and gorilla groups under study confirmed that they differed in their social interaction rates. Our findings showed that chimpanzees engaged in more events of defensive support and spent much more time in close physical contact and grooming interactions compared to the lowland gorillas.

These results are consistent with many previous findings. For example, several studies focusing on post-conflict interactions demonstrated that reconciliation, a behavioral strategy used to restore the pre-existing social bonding between the aggressor and the victim, is frequent in chimps but not in gorillas.

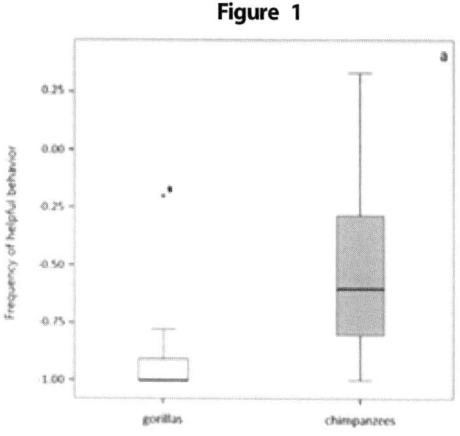

Figure 1

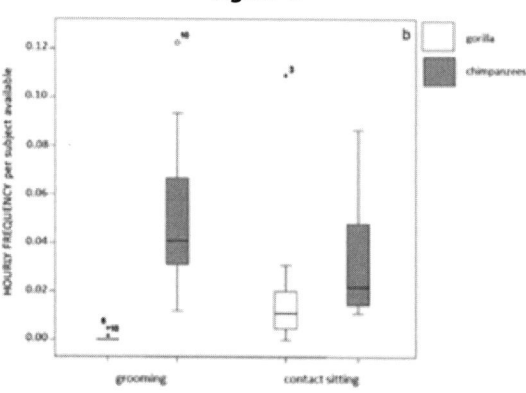

Figure 2

Figures adapted from "Differences in play can illuminate differences in affiliation: A comparative study on chimpanzees and gorillas" by Cordoni et al., 2018.

43

Which choice best summarizes the organization of the passage?
A) A theory is advanced, then refuted later based on an experiment.
B) An analysis of a phenomenon is provided, then a discussion of its moral implications follows.
C) A particular social interaction is discussed, then social interactions among primates are detailed.
D) A set of evidence is examined, then the integrity of that evidence is questioned.

44

Which of the following best represents the author's opinion towards play?
A) Play can sometimes lead to violent behavior.
B) Play is dependent on the organization of the group involved.
C) Existing theories about the short-term benefits of play are misleading.
D) Play does not differ based on characteristics and behavioral patterns of the group.

45

Which choice provides the best evidence for the answer to the previous question?
A) Lines 1-5 ("Compared...view")
B) Lines 9-12 ("It...competition")
C) Lines 13-18 ("Recent...group")
D) Lines 38-40 ("Chimpanzees...offspring")

46

As used in line 27, "retention" most nearly means
A) continuation.
B) possession.
C) confinement.
D) reservation.

47

The primary purpose of the third and fourth paragraph (lines 36-68) is to
A) identify different types of plays that chimpanzees and gorillas engage in.
B) draw a contrast between chimpanzees' social interactions and those of gorillas.
C) define complex social interactions that chimpanzees and gorillas employ.
D) emphasize the difficulty of measuring plays quantitatively.

48

Which choice provides the best evidence for the claim that lowland gorillas have less social interactions than chimpanzees do?
A) Lines 63-64 ("Adult...ways")
B) Lines 65-68 ("For example...old")
C) Lines 69-72 ("The...rates")
D) Lines 74-78 ("Our...gorillas")

49

As used in line 79, "demonstrated" most nearly means
A) manifested.
B) indicated.
C) protested.
D) authenticated.

50

According to the figures and the passage, which argument about gorillas' grooming is correct?
A) Their grooming behavior is difficult to measure.
B) Their grooming behavior is similar to that of chimpanzees.
C) Their grooming behavior occurs more frequently than contact sitting.
D) Their grooming behavior is almost nonexistent.

51

Which choice best describes the data presented in figure 1?
A) The median frequency of helpful behaviors for gorillas is much lower than that of chimpanzees.
B) Chimpanzees and gorillas have similar median frequencies of helpful behaviors.
C) Chimpanzees' frequency of helpful behaviors is higher for adult chimpanzees.
D) The frequency of helpful behaviors for gorillas is lower for adult gorillas.

52

Which statement is best supported by both figures and the passage?
A) Gorillas tend to behave more aggressively towards offsprings than adults.
B) Gorillas enjoy less frequent but more significant social interactions among themselves than chimpanzees do.
C) Play during adulthood is more beneficial than play during childhood for both gorillas and chimpanzees.
D) On average, chimpanzees demonstrate more supportive social behaviors among themselves than gorillas do.

STOP

If you finish before time is called, you may check your work on this section only.
Do not turn to any other section.

Part 1

Practice Test 4: Answer Key and Explanations

Reading Test 4 Answer Key

Reading Test 4 Question	Answer
1	B
2	C
3	D
4	A
5	A
6	A
7	A
8	B
9	C
10	A
11	B
12	B
13	A
14	D
15	B
16	A
17	C
18	A
19	C
20	A
21	D
22	B
23	B
24	A
25	A
26	C

Reading Test 4 Question	Answer
27	A
28	B
29	D
30	B
31	D
32	D
33	C
34	A
35	B
36	B
37	D
38	D
39	B
40	C
41	A
42	C
43	C
44	B
45	C
46	A
47	B
48	D
49	B
50	D
51	A
52	D

*For self-scoring assessment tables, please turn to page 189.

passage 1

1

A) Y Although the passage is indeed a "humorous" story depicting a delusional Don Quixote, there is no evidence that "lady Dulcinea" is a noble lady.

B) **ANSWER: The passage's main character, Don Quixote, is indeed a character who is deeply delusionary abou t his status and reality; this is revealed in the passage by the initial reaction of the landlord and the observations made by the onlookers. The innkeeper skillfully lets Don Quixote go on with his delusions in order to have some fun, but his actions result in a spontaneous fight between a carrier and Don Quixote. The carrier faints after being hit by Don Quixote's lance.**

C) Y Don Quixote, the main character, is a knight only in his delusions; the landlord is therefore not his lord, and no ceremony takes place at all. This question would be correct only if the question had asked about Don Quixote's own perception of the events that took place.

D) NM-Opp There is no comedic play that takes place, as Don Quixote is not an actor; while Don Quixote refers to lady Dulcinea during his fight with the carrier, the latter is not even aware of the so-called lady's existence.

2

A) "boon" cannot be a "detriment" in any circumstances; the landlord would be providing help to Don Quixote by giving a boon.

B) "compensation" refers to something given for past equivalent. It doesn't fit the context where the landlord has not done any wrong to nor received something from Don Quxiote to justify a "compensation"

C) **ANSWER: "Boon," by definition, refers to something that is helpful. In this case, the landlord would be providing a "boon," or "benefaction," to Don Quixote if he accepts him into the inn.**

D) "prosperity" is so nebulous a term that does not fit here.

3

A) "considered" is not a synonym to "proved"; it also does not fit the context where the meaning has to be "shown".

B) the landlord did not "evaluate" anything; through his adventures, he had simply "shown" proof to the world that he was physically capable.

C) "hardened" neither fits the context nor is a synonym to "proved".

D) **ANSWER Taking the context into account, this is the correct answer. The landlord, in his imagined past, had "shown", "proven", or "demonstrated" his physical prowess through his adventures.**

4

A) **ANSWER: In the 2nd paragraph, the landlord decides to not treat Don Quixote as an outright lunatic and to play along with Don Quixote's delusions. He does this so he can "make sport of the night" (lines 26-27).**

B) NI The landlord only tells the story after deciding to pretend to believe in Don Quixote. This is not the reason, only the result.

C) NM While the landlord does indeed realize that Don Quixote may not be mentally sound, he is not worried about him, he merely wishes to have fun.

D) NM There is no mention that the landlord wants to help Don Quitoxe's overcome his delusions.

5

A) **ANSWER: (Lines 23-28) These lines illustrate the landlord's train of thought, and his decision to have fun with Don Quixote's illusions.**

B) NI These lines show the result of, not the evidence of, the landlord's decision to pretend-believe, and is thus wrong.

C) NI These lines depict the landlord's probably fictional adventures; thus, it is wrong.

D) NI Somewhat like 5C, these lines illustrate the purported reason why the landlord is accepting Don Quixote into his "castle", which is his inn. The real reason why the landlord pretends to believe the main character has already been established, so this answer choice is thus wrong.

6

A) **ANSWER: After the landlord pretends to believe Don Quixote, it is mentioned in lines 45-47 that Don Quixote "promises to follow" the landlord's "advice scrupulously"; it is subsequently mentioned that it was arranged that he "should watch his armour". Thus, A is correct.**

B) NM There is no mention of Don Quixote wishing to avoid payment; this answer is outright incorrect.

C) NM, NI Although Don Quixote is indeed following the landlord's "advice", this is not done to avoid offending the landlord.

D) NI While lady Dulcinea is indeed referred to in the passage, the part about her only appears when Don Quixote is quarrelling with a carrier, which is much later in the passage than the part where Don Quixote guards his armour.

7

A) **ANSWER: The scenery that Don Quixote makes in lines 59-64 draws many people to observe Don Quixote, "a form of madness"; the various postures that Don Quixote makes strikes people as being very odd. Thus, A is correct.**

B) NM The passage does not in any way mention the number of people in the village.

C) NI The lines do not mention whether Don Quixote completed his exercises with "skill."

D) NM Although the crowd indeed regards Don Quixote as absurd, it is not implied anywhere that they are horrified.

8

A) NI While Don Quixote indeed mentions lady Dulcinea, he is merely seeking out her protection and aid; he is not declaring his love for her (his love for her has already been established, according to Don Quixote)

B) **ANSWER: Don Quixote regards the carrier's**

action as a direct challenge to him; thus, he attempts to bring his lady's luck to him, preaching out to her in thoughts to not abandon him in his first impending battle.

C) NI While lady Dulcinea is mentioned, Don Quixote is not recalling his encounter with lady Dulcinea; he is focused on the carrier he perceives as having challenged him.

D) NM There is no mention of Don Quixote's "most important consideration as a knight," so there is no evidence that backs up this answer choice.

9

A) while "amazed" is a synonym to "stunned", in this context, it is plain that the carrier was literally "stunned" and was unable to compose himself due to being hit by a lance. Thus, "stunned" was not used to convey the sense of surprise in this case.

B) Like 9B, speechless is often used to demonstrate surprise: i.e. situations where a person is surprised to an extent that he was "speechless"; the element of surprise does not fit into the passage's context.

C) **ANSWER: As it is obvious that the carrier in the passage almost passed out after being hit by Don Quixote and cannot compose himself, it would be fitting to say that stunned was used to illustrate that he was "disoriented".**

D) while "startled" has an element of surprise and hints that the person who was "startled" was surprised in an unexpected, even in a negative way (unlike amazed which has somewhat a positive connotation), the carrier was not simply startled; he was stunned due to being hit.

10

A) **ANSWER: In the passage, the carrier attempts to get water from the trough, but Don Quixote's armour is in the way; thus he is forced to move away the armour (despite Don Quixote's protest), resulting in Don Quixote slamming the carrier with his lance.**

B) NI, 2Str While the carrier had indeed disregarded Don Quixote's request to leave his armour untouched, it is shown in the passage that he was merely trying to continue on with his duties as a carrier. While Don Quixote may regard the carrier's touching of the armour as a move to beliitle him, the carrier probably would not have had such an intention.

C) NM There is no mention in the passage that the carrier insulted (or even knows) lady Dulcinea.

D) NM There is no reference to an attempt by the carrier to steal Don Quixote's sword.

11

A) While Don Quixote's armour and the carrier are both mentioned, the carrier had not yet physically removed Don Quixote's armour at this point of the passage.

B) **ANSWER: (Lines 75-81) These lines illustrate how the carrier, disregarding Don Quixote's stern warning, moves the armour away from the trough to continue on with his duty.**

C) NI These lines illustrate Don Quixote's reaction to the removal of his armour, not the actual part of the removal.

D) NI Consequence of the removal of the armour, not the actual illustration of how the carrier removes the armour.

passage 2

12

A) Y-NI While the initial part of the passage indeed deals with current conflicts in a given area, the latter part is not focused on detailing the damages done on the companies due to it; thus, this choice is wrong.

B) **ANSWER: This is the answer as there is a shift in the main focus from describing conflicts involving oil, agriculture, and pastoralism in several countries in Africa to suggestions about potential solutions starting with line 61.**

C) NM-NI The global oil industry not the prime focus of the passage; the focus is the conflict between it and pastoralism.

D) NM-NI The first part of the passage is not discussing the history of pastoralism, so this answer choice is wrong.

13

A) **ANSWER: possibility fits with viability as the passage refers to commercial "viability" of using—or the possibility of exploiting—Tullow oil.**

B) Liveliness does not share the meaning of "viability" used in the context.

C) While "viability" can indeed mean "life" and is similar to energy in a certain context, this is not the case here.

D) Impulse as a meaning does not fit in the context where "viability" was used to define "feasibility".

14

A) Opp While the author acknowledges that African governments argue that pastoralism is representative of the backwardness of Africa, it is evident that the author does not share this view.

B) NM There is no mention in the passage that states or implies that pastoralism cannot be adopted in other continents besides Africa.

C) Opp The passage mentions how pastoralism is harmed by the oil industry.

D) **ANSWER: The passage states that governments view pastoralism as something that is backward and primitive, resulting in discrimination of pastoral communities.**

15

A) While choice A states that pastoralism is viewed by the local governments as "primitive", it does not actually describe directly that the governments are pursuing policies to inhibit pastoralism in the region.

B) **ANSWER: (lines 13 - 16) This is the correct line evidence as the lines directly state how the government of Kenya has restricted pastoral mobility.**

C) cannot be the answer as the lines are simply referring to how the oil industry can have ambivalent results on pastoralism in Africa.

D) simply states that oil industry has become an additional worry for Sudanese pastoralists, and hence cannot be the answer.

16

A) ANSWER: Right after beginning the paragraph with the contrast word, "but", the author goes on in these lines stating that infrastructure and road conditions have improved thanks to the development of the oil industry. This is the best evidence.

B) Opp This answer choice states how the detrimental effects of oil exploitation has been well studies, completely opposite of evidence necessary for 16.

C) Opp Like 16 B, this answer choice focuses on the negative aspects of oil industry within Africa, and thus cannot be an answer.

D) NI This answer choice lists possible advice to take; it does not praise oil industry and how it has brought positive effects to the region.

17

A) Opp The question is actually posed to allude to the fact that there now could be answers; it is not yet the point to discuss significance,

B) NM The author's initial point is discussion about pastoralism and how it was and is prominent in AfricA)

C) ANSWER: The question was posed as an acknowledging of the author himself stating that he does not know the full extent of influence that oil industry has on pastoralism, as there have been limited research.

D) NI While the author does admit weaknesses in the oil industry, he is by no means admitting that oil industry is purely bad; he is yet to make a conclusion which will be arrived as the passage goes on.

18

A) ANSWER: choice "engender" in this context means to facilitate, to induce; in this case, therefore, "promoted" fits perfectly as an answer.

B) As engender means "entail", "induce" in the context provided in the passage, it cannot mean "evolve".

C) Inflamed has a negative connotation and has a meaning close to "incite", which does not really fit in the context here.

D) Similar to 18 C, incite does not fit in the context here where "engender" is used to mean "entail", "induce" in a neutral manner.

19

A) Y - > NI While the job of CLO is indeed to encourage communication, it is not one between the oil companies; it is between an oil company and the local populace.

B) 2Str, NM Utilizing CLOs might be a possible way of enhancing relationship between pastoral life and oil companies; it is not a panacea that would ensure the bright future of African pastoralism.

C) ANSWER: This is the correct answer as the last paragraph indeed mentions that current conflict could be managed and even perhaps be mitigated through the utilization of CLOs by oil companies.

D) NM It is not the Turkana community that is being praised here; the last paragraph paragraph merely suggests that CLOs could be utilized to mitigate the current conflicts in pastoral regions affected by oil companies.

20

A) ANSWER: The author views the current situation as "critical"; this is why he warns against inaction and even suggests possible solutions himself in order to mitigate and change the means that are being conducted at the moment. Even with these solutions, the author views the current situation as not favourable.

B) Opp, 2Str While the author suggests possible remedies to the current situation, he does not by no means view the current situation as favorable.

C) 2Gen, NI He is not neutral in considering oil companies' influence on pastoral lands, as he views that solutions must be carried out in order to actively change the current ways.

D) Opp The author is very interested in combating the current issues that plague the regions where there are both pastoralism and oil companies; he is not disinterested.

21

A) These lines are simply suggesting one possible method that could mitigate the current situation. It does not really set the tone of the passage or reveal author's analysis of the current situation.

B) These lines are simply describing in detail why and how CLOs by oil companies should and would operate.

C) These lines are merely a hint toward what policies would be beneficial for the oil companies.

D) ANSWER: This choice is correct as the lines suggest that the author believes it will be very difficult to address the current situation in Africa, Kenya. This illustrates the critical nature of the current situation.

22

A) NM Demand for low, unskilled labor and dividing revenue between the companies and the government has no relationship that is described in the passage.

B) ANSWER: This is correct as starting in line 89, the passage states that if local populace could be educated and be joined as a workforce, the pros of enhancing reputation would outweigh the cons of training for the labor.

C) NM The benefit of governmental regulation of the workforce was not mentioned in the passage, and hence this answer choice is wrong.

D) NM While the author is indeed advocating for some form of an "understanding" between the local populace who practice pastoralism and the oil companies, this does not entail the latter promoting the former. Therefore, this answer choice is incorrect.

passage 3

23

A) NI Passage 1 is not arguing against the authenticity of passage 2; given a phenomenon, smartphone and IT usage, they each make different conclusions.

B) ANSWER: Passage 1 views smartphones in a negative light, citing addictions, while passage 2 is positive about effects of smartphone & social media.

C) Opp Instead of expanding, passage 1 presents an entirely different view on smartphone usage/ IT compared to that of passage 2.

D) NM Passage 1 does not elaborate on a study that is discussed in passage 2.

24

A) ANSWER: Passage 1 discusses about how using smartphone has various negative effects, and passage 2, trying to put a neutral light on controversy around smartphone usage (especially social media), discusses its social impact

B) 2Str, Y, NM While passage 2 indeed attempts to diffuse some controversy regarding smartphone/ social media use, it does not go as far as "debunking" them.

C) NI It is not possible to simply regard theories discusses in passage 1 as novel and those discussed in passage 2 as conventional.

D) Y - NI While passage 2 indeed focuses more on the psychological / social impact, passage 1 is not a general overview of smartphone usage; it is more akin to criticism of it.

25

A) ANSWER: revamp is synonym for "revolutionize", and it is hence the answer even when considering the context.

B) There's no certain object the technology is trying to "outshine" or be much better than.

C) Purpose is to revolutionize, not make it more accessible.

D) There's no certain object the technology is trying to tower above

26

A) Opp "educational" is the least likely thing that the author of passage 1 would categorize smartphone usage as.

B) Opp smartphone usage, according to passage 1, has significant deterimental effect upon its users.

C) ANSWER: As the author of passage 1 views smartphone usage as very deterimental, "lamentable" would be how the author considers the current situation regarding smartphone usage.

D) NM There is no mention of whether the author regards smartphone usage to be temporal or not.

27

A) ANSWER: After making concession that whether smartphone usage can be classified as an actual addiction is not entirely decided, the author nonetheless refutes right after with strong argumentative style. Hence, these lines would be considered as persuasive.

B) 2Str The word "definite" is too strong to make this answer choice correct.

C) Opp There is no "reluctance" that can be felt in the author's argument described in these lines.

D) NI This is more of the author's argument, or declaration, than an emotional plea.

28

A) NI the "changed conditions" is not addressing "differing identities" of those who utilize social media; it is how the social media is utilized itself.

B) **ANSWER: This would be the answer as it directly states that social media usage has been diversified and that it is the issue.**

C) NI The lines are not discussing about the deterimental effects from changing social media usage.

D) NI "bias" is not discussed nor is the issue in changes in social media usage.

29

A) These lines are simply introducing the passage and people's lofty expectations about how development in informational technology may revolutionarize many things; hence, this answer choice is wrong.

B) These lines are simply stating that some overly optimistic expectations about development in IT techonology may be misfounded.

C) **ANSWER: Lines 61-63 These lines imply that unlike in the past, social media can now be used to publicly present oneself; this would be most fitting to 28B.**

D) These lines are simply elaborating on what ways one can use social media to publicly present oneself; it can be said that 29C is better as it contains the main idea.

30

A) NI There is no counterargument to a previous argument that is present in the lines 82-85.

B) **ANSWER: This answer is correct as the author successfully connects concepts that were previously utilized to describe earlier medias such as TV to novel social media.**

C) Opp Instead of refuting anything, the author is actually making an assertion in the said lines.

D) Y, NI "usefulness" of a theory has nothing to do with a new claim that author makes in the lines 82-85.

31

A) 2Gen, NI These lines do not contain any mention or hint about social media aiding young people establish their identity. Considering that these lines are from passage 1, which denounces smartphone usage, this can be anticipated to an extent.

B) NI These lines do not contain any mention or hint about social media aiding young people establish their identity. Considering that these lines are from passage 1, which denounces smartphone usage, this can be anticipated to an extent.

C) NI These lines are stating that the notion that social media and IT development would revolutionize everything is naive at best.

D) **ANSWER: These lines indeed state that people, which would include those who are young, can have "development of social identity" through connecting online.**

32

A) Y - 2Str, NM While the author of passage 1 would indeed be alarmed, as he is cautious and views smartphone usage negatively, he didn't classify it as one of the "known causes of social media addiction"; this would be extreme.

B) Y, NM Like 32A, the word choice "dangerous" neither is mentioned nor matches the argument of passage 1.

C) Opp Passage 1 would not find such practice interesting; the author would be guarding against it.

D) **ANSWER: The author would regard this practice with concern, and state that such behavior may be exemplary of "problematic smartphone use".**

passage 4

33

A) NM - "multiple types of governments" is the danger phrase, as this is not in the passage.

B) NI - "disbanding enemies" are the danger words, as this is not the objective.

C) **ANSWER: unity is the central message in this speech.**

D) NI - "international trade" are the danger words, because this is not the main idea.

34

A) **ANSWER: The central distinction is the different economies of the North and South.**

B) NM - "transportation" is the danger word, as it is not in the passage.

C) NM - "against international trade" is the danger phrase, the passage does not say that the South is against trade.

D) OPP - "North cultivates crops" Actually, the South cultivates crops.

35

A) This choice fails when it is plugged into the sentence.

B) **ANSWER: "to draw" means to gather, which should be our guess word.**

C) To summarize means to make brief, which does not fit with attention.

D) To purify is to clean, which does not fit with attention.

36

A) NM - "expansion" is the danger word, as it is not in the passage.

B) **ANSWER: referring to previous paragraph and commerce**

C) OPP - "control" is the danger word, as Washington suggests a republican government and less government control (lines 55-59), not more.

D) 2Str - Washington advocates different types of economies but not "cultures."

37

A) NI No promotion is given here.

B) NI A bond is mentioned, but there is no promotion here.

C) NI Motivation is given, but what unity promotes is not here.

D) **ANSWER: The lines refer to trade, which is promoted by unity.**

38

A) NM - "past" is the danger word, as Washington is not referring to the past.

B) NI - "different nations" are the danger words, as Washington is interested in the union, not other countries.

C) 2Str - Washington stresses unity, but warning against a possible civil war is far too strong.

D) **ANSWER: These lines emphasize the benefits that a union will bring.**

39

A) "permanent" is not a synonym of "hostile"

B) **ANSWER: We are looking for a word that means "against," so this is the best choice.**

C) "Bitter" contains a negative emotion, which should not be introduced.

D) "indifferent" is not a synonym of "hostile"

40

A) NM - "colonizing" is the danger word, as it is not in the passage.

B) NM - "neglects its allies abroad" is the danger phrase, because there is no mention of neglecting allies.

C) **ANSWER: "those broils" in line 51 refer to wars in foreign nations, and Washington insists that America as a union should not get involved in them.**

D) OPP - "upkeep its military" is the danger phrase, as Washington argues against overgrown military establishments (lines 56-57).

41

A) NI - "risks" is the danger word, because experience cannot solve risks.

B) **ANSWER: This choice answers Washington's preceding rhetorical question**

C) NM - "current outrage" is the danger phrase, because outrage does not exist in the text.

D) NM - "history" is not in the passage.

42

A) NI: These lines deal with the interaction between the East and West, which is not what the question is asking.

B) NI: Washington suggests what the union must do, not what individual citizens must do.

C) **ANSWER: "every reflecting and virtuous mind" - These lines introduce the individual, and the preservation of the Union as the top patriotic desire.**

D) NI: These lines send a hopeful message on the organization of the central government, but do not suggest what a citizen must do.

passage 5

43

A) NM: "experiment" is the danger word, and there is

no experiment that later "refutes" (also a danger word).

B) NM: "moral implications" is the danger word, and not mentioned.

C) ANSWER: **The social interaction "play" is introduced, followed by a study of primates. This is the best choice.**

D) NM: "integrity of that evidence" is dangerous, and not mentioned. Similar to B in the sense that both answer choices steer the test taker towards some kind of ethical judgment.

44

A) Opp: "violent" is the danger word, and if anything, it is suggested that play leads to social behavior.

B) ANSWER: **Play depends on social context and the group.**

C) NI: "misleading" is the danger word, and since the passage expands upon existing theories of play, it is not fair to label them as misleading.

D) Opp: "does not differ" is the danger word, and it is shown through the comparison of chimps and gorillas that play does differ.

45

A) NI: That play is difficult to contextualize does not help answer the previous question.

B) NI: That play has short-term benefits does not help answer the previous question.

C) ANSWER: **Play can be shaped by the social structure and the group. This is the best choice that supports the answer to the previous question.**

D) NI: Information on chimpanzee societies does not help answer the previous question.

46

A) ANSWER: **Guessing the word by context should give us "ongoing," which is closest to continuation.**

B) "possession" refers to keeping something physical, so it doesn't fit in the context of "play."

C) "confinement" is also physical, and has a negative connotation which is not suitable here.

D) "reservation" doesn't fit with the idea that play continues into adulthood. Reservation can refer to hesitation (conceptual) or a literal restaurant reservation (booking a time). Neither work.

47

A) 2spc: "types of plays" is the danger word, and the passage details types of social interactions, not play

B) ANSWER: **The third paragraph introduces two primate groups, the chimpanzee and the lowland gorilla. The third paragraph analyzes chimpanzee behavior, while the fourth paragraph analyzes western lowland gorilla behavior. This is the best choice.**

C) 2str: "complex" is the danger word, and the text doesn't support the fact that interaction is complex. If anything, interactions in gorillas are practically nonexistent, so it couldn't be complex

D) NM: "difficulty" and "quantitatively" are both dangerous and unsubstantiated.

48

A) NI: The lines only deal with female lowland gorilla behavior.

B) NI: Similar to A, these lines only deal with female lowland gorilla behavior.

C) 2gen: The lines mention both chimpanzee and gorilla interaction, but fails to provide concrete evidence that gorillas have less social interaction.

D) **ANSWER: These lines provide conclusive evidence that chimpanzees exhibit greater social interaction than gorillas do.**

49

A) "manifested" is not a synonym of "demonstrated"

B) **ANSWER: Guessing the answer should give us "showed," which is closest to indicated. This is the best choice.**

C) Studies can't protest.

D) 2str: authenticate is a bit of a stretch.

50

A) NI/NM: "difficult to measure" is off topic, since such difficulties are not discussed in the passage

B) opp: "similar" is incorrect.

C) opp: "more frequently" is incorrect.

D) **ANSWER: This is the correct interpretation of the graphs and the passage.**

51

A) **ANSWER: This is the best interpretation of the graph.**

B) opp: "similar" is incorrect

C) NM: "adult" is dangerous, since the graph does not display age distributions

D) NM: same issue as C.

52

A) NM: "offspring" refers to age, so similar problem with 51 C and 51 D

B) 2gen: "more significant" hmm...what does that even mean. We can't peer into gorillas and how they think, so it is hard to say which interaction is more significant.

C) NM: "beneficial" is the danger world, and the explanation would be similar to b. What is "more beneficial?" the passage and graph do not clarify.

D) **ANSWER: This is the best interpretation of the graphs and the conclusion drawn in the passage.**

Raw Score Conversion Chart

Raw Score (# of correct answers)	Reading Section Score	Raw Score (# of correct answers)	Reading Section Score
0	100	30	280
1	100	31	280
2	100	32	290
3	110	33	290
4	120	34	300
5	130	35	300
6	140	36	310
7	150	37	310
8	150	38	320
9	160	39	320
10	170	40	330
11	170	41	330
12	180	42	340
13	190	43	350
14	190	44	350
15	200	45	360
16	200	46	370
17	210	47	370
18	210	48	380
19	220	49	380
20	220	50	390
21	230	51	400
22	230	52	400
23	240		
24	240		
25	250		
26	250		
27	260		
28	260		
29	270		

*Please note that these scores are best approximations and that actual scores on the SAT may slightly vary, depending on individual adaptations made by the College Board.

Contributors

Written and edited by the talented test prep professionals at
PaulAcademy

PaulAcademy is the publishing arm of one of the industry-leading test prep organizations in Asia. PaulAcademy is a dedicated test prep organization that has helped thousands of students to realize their potentials and achieve their dreams. As a leader in test prep & strategy development specializing in SAT, ACT and AP preparation, PaulAcademy teaches pragmatic problem-solving skills that will ultimately help students obtain successful academic results. PaulAcademy aims to spread its expert knowledge to students worldwide.

Editor-in-Chief
Paul Kim

Head of Publishing
Niles Bliss

Material Development & Editing
Junhee Lee, Jennifer Ryu, Patrick Kim, Hyunseung Yang

Email: books@paulacademy.net   Website: http://www.paulacademy.net

Copyright © 2019 All rights reserved by PaulAcademy.
The contents of the book may not be copied or reused without the express written consent of PaulAcademy.

SAT® is a registered trademark of the College Board, which is not affiliated with and does not endorse this product.

ISBN : 979-11-86461-22-8